BOOK ENDO

When I think of my friend Ben, two words come to my mind--- Golf and God. I've never met a man who loves and follows the principles that are set forth in each discipline like Ben. In golf, he follows all the rules on the course, and in his life, he follows God's teachings to the best of his ability, always with a smile on his face. In his book, Ben has an unbelievable talent to explain many of life's situations in beautifully written poetic prose. Good job Ben!

- Dick Couey, Waco, Texas, author of over thirty books on physiology, nutrition, and sports medicine. He is an "age-shooter" in golf and wants you to serve God longer in good health.

Ben Hagins is a masterful communicator. His winsome style is most appreciated by those willing to read and reflect on his words while sitting in an easy chair around the fireplace with a cup of coffee in hand. His life stories and accompanying poems touch both the mind and heart of the reader. Enjoy!
-Dr. Randy Marshall, Pastor, White Bluff Chapel, Whitney, Texas.

Ben Hagins' infectious faith, love for people, and zeal for life, shine through everything he writes. He is, above all, an "Encourager." He knows how to inspire others to reach higher and deeper when they face troubles or take on new challenges.
-Dr. Paul Sands, Pastor, First Woodway Baptist Church, Waco, Texas

Jo,   Sep '24

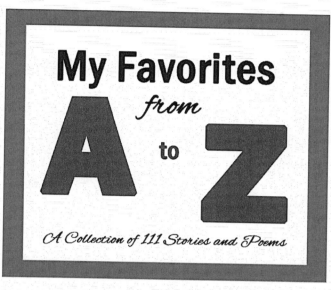

My Favorites *from* A to Z

A Collection of 111 Stories and Poems

BEN HAGINS

You + Cookie are some
of my favorites.
He was such a supporter
of Links Fellowship.

R/L

Sic 'em, Ben + Kathy

My Favorites from A to Z

© Copyright 2024 Ben Hagins
ISBN: 978-1-962848-17-6

Editing and Design: Marji Laine
Cover image: Ben Hagins

 Published by:
Roaring Lambs Publishing
17110 Dallas Parkway, Suite 260
Dallas, TX 75248

Published in the United States of America.

DEDICATION

To my faithful and loving wife, Kathy,
who married me after only three dates.
We knew our marriage was made in Heaven.

Thank you for giving me space
to work, play, and "do my thing."

I will love you forever.

CONTENTS

Ben Hagins

Ben Hagins

INTRODUCTION

I had never written a poem in my life until the night we moved into our "get-away" place that we named "Slice of Heaven," which became the title of my first book.

That special night began my poetry career, and on future trips to our "Slice of Heaven," I would continue this writing based on actual situations.

I've now written over 500 poems. Please enjoy 111 of my favorites.

I WANT MY "GRANDS" TO KNOW

If I were sitting in my grandfather's lap, what would I want him to say to me? Would I have time for him? I want to say yes, but if my "grands" are like me, I'd better be ready for a short visit. They are both very busy. Both Robert and Kate Hagins, call me, "Big Pardner." I called my dad, "Pardner," and he always had time for me.

As far as legacy is concerned, I want my "grands" to know the following several things about the family history, accomplishments, and spiritual background.

My dad, Charlie Hagins, and their great-grandfather was taken from me way too early. My dad was killed in a tragic shooting incident just before his age 65, in 1978. My mom, Lucie Hagins, despite this setback, faithfully served as church secretary and was active in all community projects in Fordyce, Arkansas. They both practiced stewardship and prepared me for a future thirty-year career in financial planning.

My wife, Kathy, had parents that were also very special. Her mom, Sarah Price, had a severe stroke in her mid-forties. Her positive attitude, even with this adversity, was a testament to her example of strength. Her husband, Jeff Price, faithfully cared for her both physically and financially despite this hardship. They lived in Jonesboro, Arkansas, and what an example for my "grands" to learn from!

I want my "grands" to know that I served my country in the U.S. Air Force, mostly in the B-52 program. This career lasted almost ten years as I left the military after my dad's death in 1978. While in the service, Kathy and I started a financial program with a company that I would later serve. This foundation led to a second career in the financial services industry. I want my "grands" to learn that there are no get-rich quick schemes, but through smart savings, planning, and working a diversified portfolio, they can be financially prepared for their future.

My wife of over fifty years is my "gift from heaven." I met Kathy in the San Francisco airport after her two-year tour of service as a teacher with the International Mission Board.

We had a whirlwind romance, marrying after only three dates over six months. Then, three days into our honeymoon, we had a near fatal accident. Our car was totaled, yet we were spared with no injuries. Was there a providential God looking over us? I think so. Kathy, I pledge my love to you forever.

Finally, I want our "grands" to know about our Christian beliefs. We both grew up in Christian homes. What an important foundation to build upon and now in our retirement years, to have around us such solid churches with worthwhile programs.

Our legacy is still growing. About twenty-five years ago, I started writing poetry when the Spirit led me. My first poem was written after we completed building our small lake home, called Slice of Heaven. It's one of my favorites, titled—Back Deck.

In conclusion, I can think of no finer legacy to leave my "grands" than written words about our family's history, accomplishments, and spiritual background. My motto for my "grands" continues to be: "Learn something new every day!"

Ben Hagins

MY FAVORITES

I've been composing my second book for about ten years since my first book, "Slice of Heaven," was published in 2014.

The reason—I've probably completed over 500 poems and thoughts about my life experiences, nearly all from a faith perspective. I believe I've written enough to complete book #2.

I had spoken several times to my grands' classes during poetry week and to my Christian Writers Workshop. For those classes, I put about twenty poems on the whiteboard and then asked my group to choose from that list for the story and poem they want to hear.

I would usually open with this statement, "Now this is one of my favorites."

After a few times of repeating this statement and going over the poem and the reason behind the poem, the class would say, "We know Mr. Ben, this is one of your favorites."

MY FAVORITES

Talk to me, Lord, on this winter day.
Just what is it that you want me to say?

I do believe in that still small voice
Because you've given me that power of choice.

Do I play, read, or write? Just what should I do?
The answer might depend on if I would listen to you.

But then it's up to me to decide my plan.
When I follow your way, I just know I can

Complete my goal and finish my book.
The title—

MY FAVORITES FROM A - Z.

Who will take a look?

Ben Hagins

A

Ben Hagins

AS A RULE

This poem got my attention when I was going through my mom's—Lucie Hagins—belongings after her death in March 2008. She told me this small-framed poem was on the wall of my grandad's drugstore in Fordyce, Arkansas, and it's on my office wall at home now.

I later added the last line for emphasis, that we should be content with the many things we have and enjoy.

Hebrews 13:5 reminds us to live free from the love of money, and just be content. In fact, this entire chapter is about good advice, and obviously, one of my favorites.

As a rule—man's a fool,
When it's hot—he wants it cool.
When it's cool—he wants it hot,
Always wanting what is not.
Never satisfied with what he's got!

AWE

My favorite word is found in Luke,
Chapter 8, verse 25.

This word is—"AWE," which means amazement.
It made the disciples come alive.

Their faith was strengthened, and they saw the power
As Jesus calmed the storm.

He awoke from his nap and rebuked the wind.
Jesus didn't follow the norm.

For His ways were different. He had authority.
His parables taught the Word.

They were filled with knowledge, full of wisdom and
"AWE."

This message— I trust you've heard.

Ben Hagins

AIRMEN, SEAMEN, SOLDIERS, AND MARINES

Over thirty years ago, I began writing poetry. At that time, I was working as a financial advisor serving military families. Prior to that, I spent almost ten years on active duty in the U.S. Air Force, mostly in the B-52 program.

I recently read an article in James Dobson's, "Focus on the Family," magazine. A story there inspired me to write this poem about the military, one of my favorites!

AIRMEN, SEAMEN, SOLDIERS, AND MARINES

During these difficult times, the world is unsure.
Our troops are deployed. How do they endure
The stress, the strain, the mental pain,
Separation from family? What is their gain?

Is it glory, reward, a job well done,
Or duty to country that is second to none?
I think you'll agree that it's good to be free.
We're very proud that they're all they can be.

They've raised their hands in proud salute
To give lives, if required, in humble resolute.
You see, these patriots have answered the call
To protect our freedom for one and for all.

Let's not forget what all this means—
these Airmen, Seamen, Soldiers, and Marines.

ASK

Luke 11:9-10 says to "ask." It suggests that there are three levels to prayer. You can use these three letters to—A—ASK, S—Seek, and K—Knock.

The first letter—A—"Ask"—is the simplest. James 1:5 says our Lord will give liberally to all who ask.

The second letter—S —tells me to "Seek." This is more of a process and includes searching and usually takes time.

The third letter—K —is "Knock." Not all knocking is answered quickly and requires repetition. Continuing to knock can result in a door being open for you and others.

Remember this acrostic—A-S-K. As you probably have guessed, the following poem is one of my favorites.

ASK

Why did we have so much time yesteryear
When things seemed so easy and slow,

And not the busyness of today,
Always wanting to hurry-up and go?

Have to do this, have to do that. It just won't stop!
Seems there's no time in the day.

Well, I've got an answer. It just might help
To start each morning this way:

Schedule a time with Him, your Lord.
It's hard, but I know you can.

Look at the words in A-S-K—Ask, Seek, Knock.
It's in Revelation 3:20. Make this your daily plan!

Ben Hagins

ANNIVERSARY #50

Kathy Hagins and I were married on Saturday, 15 April 1972, the only day and weekend I had off that year when I was in the U.S. Air Force.

It's #50, 15 April 2022,
Been in Waco over ten years.
I would like to go more with you.

You're the only one with whom
I want to make this journey.
And thank you so much, my honey,
For allowing me another tourney.

For golf's my outlet to get outside
And chase those little balls.
But slow me down and let me know
When our "Slice of Heaven" calls.

Then we will go to rest and renew.
Will we leave this home? No, never,
Only with you, I want to be.
Just know, I will love you forever!

Ben Hagins

ABUNDANT LIFE

I always liked that part of the verse in John 10:10—
the abundant life. Our Lord has plans for each of us.
Do you believe this? One of my favorites, Proverbs
3:5-6, says all we must do is live by these words and
be transformed by the renewal of our minds, not
relying on our own understanding, but
acknowledging Him, and our paths will be straight.
Please enjoy one of my favorite poems about this
abundant life.

It's so quiet right now at my "Slice of Heaven" home.
This place is speaking to me.

With the sights and sounds and beauty that is here,
I wonder why so many can't see

That we are all put here for a purposeful life
To find our place of service to give.

If you look beyond your earthly desires,
Then the abundant life you'll live.

A STORM IS COMING

What do you do when a storm is coming?
How do you prepare?
Most people do nothing and take their chances. I
wonder if they really care.

Because nature is no respecter of persons,
calamity can happen anywhere,
Anytime, and any place.
Sometimes life doesn't seem fair.

When you hear from a friend in need,
something like this you usually say,
"I'm thinking of you with my thoughts and prayers.
What can I do today?"

But let's be truthful. We're not in their shoes.
It's hard to know what to do.
Their adversity is real. They need support.
The answer - it just might be YOU!

Give those precious gifts
—time and an understanding heart.
When you learn about a friend with problems,
take action and do your part!

Ben Hagins

ADVICE

Advice is guidance and recommendations made for prudent future action.

Why is it that young children seem to ignore their parents' words about this topic? Why do we have to learn from our mistakes and not know what to do the first time?

Proverbs 3:5-6 says it clearly. These verses are some of the most quoted in the Bible. These incredible truths will challenge you all through your life.

It is Godly wisdom and the best advice that will speak directly to your heart.

ADVICE

Trust in the Lord with all your heart.
Depend on Him in all your ways.

Do not rely on yourself, but seek His will
For all your earthly days.

Now these are words
of understanding and knowledge
Available to all who seek

These wise sayings from the good King Solomon
Will keep you from being weak.

Always be strong with truth and wisdom,
Following your Master's call.

Then abundant life is yours
from these words in Proverbs.
It's simply good advice for all.

Ben Hagins

AMEN

Since retirement, I have become an early riser, usually getting up around five o'clock in the morning. I enjoy my meditation and quiet time with my cup of coffee, while Kathy gets her restful sleep without hearing my snoring.

This particular time, our faithful dog Maddi, whom we adopted in August of 2016, was with me in my lap on our back deck. The sun was rising, showcasing my canyon, and the weather was perfect.

I composed this poem, reflecting on the words of Psalms 8:3-4.

What a morning!

AMEN

Up early this morning at my "get-away" place,
It's so quiet you can hear your heartbeat.

My faithful dog companion is right by my side,
While my wife is getting restful sleep.

The sights and sounds from my canyon out back
Are speaking directly to me.

With my pencil and pad I will try to capture
This magnificent picture I see.

Our creation was formed countless ages ago.
How did this beauty all begin?

With childlike faith as a start,
and the "Good Book" as my guide,
Is that enough for me to get an "Amen"!

B

BEST DAY

A few years ago, our Christian Writers Workshop gave an assignment to describe one of the following: your worst, best, good, or bad day. I chose my best day, and it was Tax Day, Saturday, 15 April 1972, my wedding day over fifty years ago.

But the story starts a little earlier. The previous summer, I was on active duty in California with the U.S. Air Force, after five years at Baylor University, and very single. I was called a few months earlier by my dad's older brother, Tom Hagins, and "ordered" to be in San Francisco to meet an airplane with Kathy Price returning from overseas where she had served a two-year program with the International Mission Board.

As I waited to greet this set-up/blind-date/arranged meeting, I reticently wondered what this young lady would be like. Kathy was the daughter of Jeff and Sarah Price from Jonesboro, Arkansas. Sarah was Uncle Tom's college close friend, and they stayed in touch through reunions, phone calls, and letters after graduating from Ouachita Baptist University in the mid-1930s.

When Kathy appeared at the arrival gate, it was love

Ben Hagins

at first sight! We were engaged the following Christmas season and married on the only Saturday I had off in 1972.

It was a beautiful weekend, and we packed the First Baptist Church with all her friends and all my Baylor fraternity brothers, along with both sets of parents who wondered how all this happened so quickly. It truly was a whirlwind romance and a marriage "made in heaven."

After reading this assignment in our workshop, I just knew I would write about my best day, being Saturday, 15 April 1972, our wedding day over fifty years ago.

BEST DAY

OKAY, GOOD, BETTER, and BEST.

Let's put these four words to the test.

When OKAY becomes GOOD,

Then GOOD can get BETTER,

Finally, BETTER can become the BEST!

Note: A few years ago, there was a series of commercials on all channels using the word—okay—to describe how one's day is going, which was not something to be desired, and was reflected in the faces of those who were hearing this response to their questions.

Hopefully, this poem will cause us to be the BEST in all we do.

BEN HAGINS

My mom, Lucie Hagins, taught me a lot about writing. I learned much more about her writing style when going through her many papers after she died at age eighty-nine in March 2008.

Many times, she would use the acrostic example. It didn't matter how many letters she would use, but this style always made a point for the different programs in her church, community activities, and civic club projects.

Mom would use that first letter and tell a brief story, so I decided to use this in my book as an example. This acrostic format was used as a writing project in our Christian Writers Workshop a few years ago. We were asked to use the first letters of our names and relate something of our writing experiences. So, here it is.

It's one of my favorite memories of Mom's writing, and I hope you like it and learn from it.

BEN HAGINS

B—Begin your writing—now!

E—Enjoy this process.

N—Never let it be said you did not try.

H—Help is always available if you seek it.

A—Always take notes on sermons and in classes.

G—Give it your best and you won't be sorry.

I—Imagine you have finished your work.

N—Now, isn't that a good feeling?

S—Sow your seeds of writing. Your family will appreciate it someday.

BACK DECK

I must say that this poem is probably my all-time favorite. The reason—it was the first one I wrote the night we moved into our "Slice of Heaven" home on Lake Whitney. It was also the hottest day of that year in July 1998.

Kathy had just gone to bed after an exhausting day of moving, but thankfully we had Trey, a Baylor junior, and two of his friends to do the heavy lifting. That evening was so peaceful and with that moon rising over the lake. The setting was just serene, and caused me to become thankful, once again, for what we had accomplished in the previous year.

This poem wasn't even planned—it just came to me and flowed onto the paper. As I reread the poem numerous times those next few days—it just continued to become meaningful to me, to the point of causing me to memorize these words.

Even now, each time I visit our back deck, look out over our canyon, and view the uninhabited acreage across the way and those Lake Whitney views, I sense my Lord's presence and creations.

In Psalms, we are reminded about the heavens, the work of His fingers, the moon and the stars which He has put in place. "What is mankind that You are mindful of them, human beings that You care for them?" (Psalm 8:4).

I continue to be thankful for this property and pray that my family will always share this with their friends, as Kathy and I will someday pass this on to them and their future families.

BACK DECK

On my back deck in my old rocking chair,
It's so quiet you can hear your heartbeat.
The stars in the heavens, the moon's on the rise.
I'd say I had the best seat

To think about God and all that he's made,
To just appreciate the fact that I'm here.
My wife's by my side, through thick and through thin,
And my son's down the road pretty near.

We've just moved into our get-away place
Never thought all of this could be.
But when you dream, and you pray,
and never give up,
The plans that you've made, you'll see

Come together for good, for all my friends,
A retreat from a too-busy day.
On my back deck, slow down and be still,
This reward, at any price, you'll pay.

Ben Hagins

BIRDS IN THE AIR

What a spectacle that came my way on this overcast day in late summer a few years ago. Hundreds of snow-white doves flew up my canyon from Lake Whitney at our "Slice of Heaven."

The morning was so peaceful and suddenly, droves and droves of these magnificent birds just kept coming! I was most fortunate to capture, on video, these majestic creatures in flight.

What a morning I had as I relaxed out back
To a site I haven't seen before.
Hundreds of white doves flew up our canyon.
Was it over? No, there came more!

A spectacle it was, this scene to behold.
My Lord was speaking to me.
Majestic this vista became,
in every sense of the word,
Doves of peace, the picture I see.

It was reserved for me, my message from above.
I believe my Lord does share.
He sends signs and wonders to all who look up.
His creation—the birds in the air!

BAPTISM

My grandson, Robert Hagins, age nine, wrote me a note on 24 March 2012, about his decision of accepting Jesus into his heart. Shortly after that, I composed this poem on Easter Sunday. It's one of my favorites.

What a glorious Easter morning
I'm greeted with today.
Pen and paper in hand on my back porch,
Thoughts of family are coming my way.

It happens many times when I slow down,
not caught up with news.
For the day is special for my grandson.
His baptism should get worldwide views.

The decision to accept the Lord,
into his heart makes me proud.
Millions of people around the world
Don't understand our worship with heads bowed,

But right now, we acknowledge our Savior and Lord
And tell the story of why He came.
Be bold with power from above,
not ashamed to wear the Christian name.

Ben Hagins

BLUEBONNETS

The most famous bluebonnets are the Texas variety, which is the state flower.

They cover immense areas across the state and are like a blue carpet in the spring. They are the most popular wildflowers in Texas.

The shape of their petals resembles the sunbonnets worn by the pioneer women. They usually appear between March and May, and they are truly classics.

Take a picture of your children sitting among them. It's a keepsake and favorite, as is this poem of mine.

Image credit: Marji Laine

BLUEBONNETS

It's early April, springtime is here.
Bluebonnets galore—I feel so near
To a creative God, so infinite, yet real.
It's the season for new beginnings. Can you feel

The wonder, the power, the freshness in the air,
Renewal and peace? How can you not care
To acknowledge your Lord? He did make it all—
Wildflowers, mesquites, and cedars so tall.

Up the canyon cliff, they grow jutting out,
Midst colors of blue and white,
purple and pink all about.
But this one thing you remember,
like classic Shakespeare sonnets,
The Texas State flower,
our Slice of Heaven bluebonnets.

BE STILL

Recently, you may have noticed how many golfers move their heads when they putt. It is easily recognizable. Most amateurs can't wait to see where their ball is going and think they can "help" get it in the hole. The pros also do this, but they seem to hesitate, if even momentarily, to watch their putter strike their ball exactly as planned, and then watch it roll toward the hole.

One of my favorite verses is Psalm 46:10a—"Be still and know that I am God."

What a great verse and principle for life and golf, and with those first two words for putting—"Be still." In fact, try this the next time you're on the putting green. Watch the putter hit the ball, but do not peek! Listen for your ball to go in, but if it does not, say out loud where you think you missed. Then look and see if you are correct.

So, next time you are faced with a tough putt, and they all are, remember this two-word phrase—BE STILL. Be at peace, be still, keep your head down and eyes focused on your target—the ball. Complete your stroke and let the results speak for themselves. You just might be surprised at the immediate good things that will happen to you in golf, as in life.

In conclusion, several of my playing companions have asked me, especially when I hole a difficult putt, "What does 46:10 mean?"—that I have written on the top of my putter? Well, here's your chance—change the conversation and tell your story.

BE STILL

One of my favorites,
Is only two words—
This simple phrase—Be still.

When you've made this a part
Of your daily prayer
You're closer to being in God's will.

Be Still and Know That I Am GOD. Psalms 46:10

For Golfers - Keep Your Head "Still" and Know That You Will Make That Putt. Ben Hagins

Ben Hagins

BREVITY OF LIFE

How many years
Do you think you have
To live upon this earth?
Psalms 90 says
It's about seventy
From the time of your birth.

And along that way
There will be pain and trouble.
Do you believe that's a fact?
So, figure out right now
How many years you have left.
Then make a resolution and act.

Make the most of your time
Grow in strength and wisdom,
And listen to that still, small voice.
Lift up your prayers
To the Lord your God.
It really is your choice.

C

Ben Hagins

CAN YOU SEE AND HEAR GOD?

Our eyes can see about 3000 stars on a clear night, and with binoculars, we can view multitudes of stars and galaxies. Just come and look through my large telescope. In fact, there are over 100 billion galaxies with trillions of stars, planets, moons and who knows what else. It is simply incomprehensible the size and magnitude of God's creations.

Psalms 8:3-6, these four verses, speak of God's creation and power.

When I flew in the U.S. Air Force, many times I was above 30,000 feet and had numerous occasions to observe the weather and the heavens. I had a large navigational radarscope to observe the patterns of clouds and possible storms.

The rule was to avoid these potential danger areas by at least twenty miles, and once, when I strayed inside of those parameters, our crew was reminded of God's power and control.

And when you come to our "Slice of Heaven" home, you can look through my telescope and experience our God in a most unique way, one of my favorite things to do.

CAN YOU SEE AND HEAR GOD?

Some claim they can't see and hear God.
Then let me suggest this test:
Come build a fire with me.
You might agree this is best

To sit, look, and listen
And enjoy this unmistakable sound.
The flames and embers are hissing,
Crackling, and dancing all around.

Now let me ask this question
In your too-busy life.
Do you wish you could slow down and
Have a quiet time for you and your wife?

Then come visit with me.
'Cause this isn't for the weak.
You'll be stronger for this time,
And you will see and hear your God speak!

Ben Hagins

CHILDREN

Three references to children coming to Jesus are found in the books of Matthew, Mark, and Luke. I do not know when a young child reaches the age of accountability, but I believe a child can receive Christ.

The German theologian, writer, and doctor, Albert Schweitzer, was asked how children learn. His response was three ways: by example, by example, and by example. Children learn by reading our lives, not our lectures.

The following poem was written during a church service when Barbra Smith, our childhood director at First Woodway Baptist, led the baby dedication program.

CHILDREN

Jesus loves the little children,
Said let them come unto me.

Prayed for them and laid on His hands
For all the people to see.

You know Heaven belongs to them.
Better come to Him like a child.

Look it up in three similar books.
Eternity, somewhere, will last a long while.

Ben Hagins

CHRISTMAS GIFT

One of the best Christmas gifts I've received from my son is a picture scrolling screen-saver for my computers. Each picture lasts about thirty seconds and reminds me of events I've enjoyed with my family.

Many times, I will take a picture and forward it to my two grands, especially from those taken years ago. Each time they will acknowledge these memories of key events with these fun-filled reminders of our special times.

Someday, these might be shown at my funeral. They reflect selected life events and my devotion to my family.

Like pictures in our hallway, these numerous computer reminders are dearly cherished by me.

CHRISTMAS GIFT

On this mild Christmas season morn,
I'm reflecting on thoughts of the past.
My parents, who wanted the best for me,
Made memories with me that would last.

Those fun filled days in my small hometown,
My dog was so faithful to me.
Over seventy years ago, these times are
Remembered with pictures I see.

And then I grew in body and soul.
Matured from a youth to a man,
Off I go to Baylor to make my own way.
Through others I know that I can

Do about anything I set out to do.
With friends I make great connections,
And now my wife of fifty-plus years,
Is my helpmate during these Christmas reflections.

Ben Hagins

CLOSER WALK

My favorite all-time hymn is—"Just A Closer Walk with Thee."

It is a traditional gospel song frequently played at funerals. The author is unknown, but research has shown it is dated back to the mid-nineteenth century southern African American churches.

This song got my attention when watching the 1967 movie classic—Cool Hand Luke with Paul Newman, as Luke was punished and put in solitary confinement.

This song has now been recorded by over 100 artists, and I plan to use this masterpiece of lyrics at my memorial service. Please reverently absorb these outstanding words to my favorite hymn.

CLOSER WALK

I am weak, but Thou art strong;
Jesus, keep me from all wrong;
I'll be satisfied as long
As I walk, let me walk close to Thee.

Just a closer walk with Thee,
Grant it, Jesus, is my plea,
Daily walking close to Thee,
Let it be, dear Lord, let it be.

Through this world of toil and snares,
If I falter, Lord, who cares?
Who with me my burden shares?
None but Thee, dear Lord, none but Thee.

When my feeble life is o'er,
Time for me will be no more;
Guide me gently, safely o'er
To Thy kingdom shore, to Thy shore.

Ben Hagins

D&E

Ben Hagins

"D" DAY REMEMBERED—6 JUNE 2024

Eighty years ago today, over 150,000 troops landed in northern France at Normandy, in the largest amphibious military operation in history.

This famous day was known as the beginning of the end of World War II, which was less than a year later. Please don't forget the importance of this day.

By the grace of God, there go I.

"D" DAY REMEMBERED—6 JUNE 2024

Up early on this beautiful morn,
I just love this time of day.
The skies are waking up, and birds are singing.
I'm so thankful that I'm not away.

Because in a foreign land, eighty years ago,
Our troops stormed an enemy shore.
Many brave men paid the ultimate price!
Why have so many gone before?

Even now, young men go, and fight for freedom,
So we can work and play,
And get up early to enjoy these mornings.
I thank God for the American way!

Ben Hagins

DAY OF INFAMY

The bombing of Pearl Harbor was on Sunday morning, 7 December 1941. My uncle, Jim Gates, was in the service stationed in Hawaii, and survived, unlike many in his squadron.

The following day, Franklin D. Roosevelt delivered his five-minute "Day of Infamy" speech, declaring war, which started World War II.

Near the end of my college years, I spoke with my uncle and dad about a possible career in the military. These talks contributed to my joining and serving in the U.S. Air Force for approximately ten years during the 1970s.

Please go to FDR's "Day of Infamy" speech and see and hear the President's visual and spoken words.

DAY OF INFAMY

It's so quiet this morning.
Somewhat like eighty years ago.
Then all hell broke out,
Historians tell us so.

A family member was involved.
But he's long since gone,
Like those 2400 men
Who lost their lives at dawn.

On that fateful Sunday morning,
They were in it all the way.
The U.S. entered WWII—
December the seventh was that day.

Now I ask you right now,
Just between you and me,
What are your thoughts
About this "Day Of Infamy?"

Ben Hagins

DESIRES OF YOUR HEART

Chapter 37 in Psalms, forty verses strong, encourages the reader to commit themselves to the Lord.

Verse number four is the one that is quoted most. Taking delight means to find peace and fulfillment in Him.

In fact, all these verses are considered one of the most loved of David's Psalms. When we take delight in the Lord, we will find true satisfaction and worth.

For these reasons, Psalms 37:4 is one of my favorites.

DESIRES OF YOUR HEART

In Psalms 37, there is a verse.
I hope it speaks to you.

It's number 4, and not too long.
It tells what your Lord will do.

It's a pearl of wisdom, and a prayer to remember.
It's just a great place to start.

So simple, so complete, so full of advice,
About the desires of your heart.

Just take delight in these words, from God.
Commit to Him your ways.

Be still in His presence. Wait patiently for Him,
And trust Him for all your days.

Ben Hagins

DICK COUEY—HERO IN MY EYES

I am a member of a group, Christian Writers Workshop, in Waco, Texas, and have been a member for over ten years. We meet February - April and September- November and have guest speakers and writing assignments that are always helpful, informative, and inspirational.

A few years ago, our assignment was to write about a hero of mine and why. I wrote about a friend, Dr. Dick Couey, a retired Baylor professor of over thirty-seven years who has published over thirty books on physiology, nutrition, exercise, and sports medicine.

Dick was a former professional baseball player (pitcher), coach, international speaker, and age-shooter in golf.

His motto is, "Take care of yourself so you can serve God better." Dick is one of my favorites, and I hope you like my poem about him.

DICK COUEY—HERO IN MY EYES

The assignment tonight
Is to write about a hero,
And a fine one I have in mind.
His name is Dick Couey
and I met him years ago.
On a one to ten scale—he's about a nine.

He's a Baylor fan
And a scientist, in fact,
Has knowledge that's over my head.
Now Dick loves the Lord
And wants you to be healthy.
Showed me his microscope and then said,

"Ben, look at your blood
And the millions of cells.
It's inspiring and you should be awed.
Do you know you're special
And one-of-a-kind?
Now present yourself acceptable to God."

Ben Hagins

DEVOTION

My dogs have been a part of my family forever. Since elementary school, I was fortunate to have had five little companions in my life. Lucky only lasted a few weeks, as he was very sick when I found him.

Then came Bullet, a fast little terrier with me from the first through the eighth grades with no leash laws in my small hometown. He even followed me to church and received a comment from the pulpit, about coming to church more than some members!

Bogey was ours for several years during my military days in Texas. And then came Speck, with that little white dot on his black chest. He even got a poem by me upon his death with a funeral service, right where he had marked his spot, with our adopted "Naber Fam" from next door.

Now we have Maddi, whom we adopted over seven years ago. This happened because our grands said, "Kaki and Big Pardner, you should adopt a dog because you will live longer." And yes, what a constant companion and part of the family is she.

All our dogs were part of the family and were favorites of mine—perfect examples of devotion!

DEVOTION

Where can you find devotion?
Where can this be seen?
I will tell you about our pet dog, Maddi,
And this is what I mean.

Every day she is with us,
No matter how we feel.
She loves us unconditionally,
Even if we miss her meal.

Her devotion is like my God,
Always there by my side.
Just call each by name.
Both will be your guide.

Now this lesson is rather simple
And take out all the emotion.
Your Lord and your pet dog
Are perfect examples of devotion.

Ben Hagins

EASTER

Easter is a celebration of Jesus's resurrection from the dead. It has been called a "movable holiday," because it doesn't fall on a specific date every year. It occurs between 22 March and 25 April, the first Sunday following the full moon after 21 March, the vernal equinox.

It is considered the principal festival for Christians around the world. The exact origins are unknown, but Lent, observed forty days prior to Easter, is a special time of reflection and prayer. Lent represents the time Jesus spent alone prior to starting his ministry.

Like Christmas, various folk customs and traditions, such as Easter bunnies, baskets, and candy, became a standard part of this holy holiday.

Please enjoy and reflect on this important date in Christian churches with my poem about Easter. It's one of my favorites.

EASTER

Easter eggs, bunnies, candy, and such—
Most all will celebrate this day.
But there's so much more about this time
To point us toward a better way.

The season of Lent is forty days prior,
With self-reflection, service and prayer.
A time to look inward, to give us strength
And cause us to be more aware

Of just what happened
2000 years ago.
A man was dead yet came alive.
Do you believe it so?

Yes, it takes total faith,
And belief on your part.
So, experience your Easter,
And let it fill up your heart!

Ben Hagins

F

FOUR WRITING TIPS

1—YELLOW PAD

Tell your story because you should,
Pass it down, for that is good.
Your grandkids don't know just what you did,
How you worked with others, and how you lived.
One technique to use, and you'll be glad
Is to write your thoughts on a big yellow pad.

2—SPECIAL PLACE AND TIME

Early, late, whenever, and where? What is your best place and time? At my "Slice of Heaven," I have placed benches that overlook my canyon in little meditation areas that have become special to me. I even wrote a poem and narrative about this place. Part of that poem reads—

Now a nice summer breeze has come my way.
Seems God has touched my face.
Reminded once again these blessings are from Him.
I'm so thankful for my Special Place.

3—DO IT NOW

Procrastination—why do we do it? My company used to give little round wooden coins with these two words— TO IT. You then asked, "What is this?"

Answer—A ROUND TO IT. Then say, "Those that get "around to it" are the ones who "get things done."

A good friend of mine reminded me of this saying when I wanted to delay doing a project that would take an hour or so to do. He looked me straight in the eyes and said, "WHY NOT NOW?" Part of this poem reads—

You just can't finish the things you don't start.
I know you're wondering just how
Will I ever get things done and reach my goals?
Just answer this question, WHY NOT NOW?

4—SEEK GOD'S WILL OF SERVICE

On of my favorite stories is recorded in the book of Matthew where our Master praised the wise use of the servants, with their five and two talents, by saying "Well done, good, and faithful servant."

Do you remember what the Lord said to the one who buried his one talent? Jesus said, "You wicked and lazy servant." The word—Servant—is mentioned over 100 times in the Bible, so it's clear that our Lord thought service was a priority item.
How about you?

Ben Hagins

FISHERS OF MEN

I'm not a fisherman, but I have a fisherman and flag shirt that I really like to wear on patriotic holidays. I also like this poem that I found when reading my friend, David Cook's book, <u>Johnny's U.S. Open, Golf's Sacred Journey 2</u>. I don't know where he found it, but it's a "keeper," as fisherman like to say.

Lord, give me grace to catch a fish so big that even I,
When telling of it afterwards, may never need to lie.

A question I would ask you
and a truthful answer wish
Are all fishermen liars and do only liars fish?

Since a question you have asked,
and a truthful answer wish,
All men are liars—and some fish.

This account of Jesus and the fisherman is recorded in passages from Matthew, Mark, and Luke. This story is one of my favorites.

FISHERS OF MEN

Jesus taught one day from a boat
On a lake called Galilee.
He said to Simon, "Cast your net
Out in the deep water of this sea."

Simon replied that the fishing was bad,
Hadn't caught anything all night.
Jesus then said, "Let down your nets.
Everything will be all right."

When that was done, their boats were full
And this fulfilled their wish.
"From now on," Jesus said, "follow Me,
Seeking people and not the fish."

Ben Hagins

FRANKLIN POTTS

Franklin was called to his heavenly home on 9 February 2024, after battling ALS. He was a fraternity brother, professor for over fifty years, and my golf friend. Along with his brother Tom, they made quite a pair. It's a mystery why a dreadful disease like ALS can happen? But Franklin Potts handled it like the champion he was!

He was unable to walk and talk in those later stages and started writing some poetry in his last years of life. His wife, Cindy, and family even produced a book to commemorate his writings titled, A Glimpse of Heaven. Please enjoy and learn from his poem, that I was asked to read at his celebration service.

THE MAN I WANT TO BE

By Franklin Potts

I want to be a man who truly cares for others,
Who thinks of all people as sisters and brothers.

A man who is open, honest, and kind,
Who is not afraid to open his heart or his mind.

Not one who judges others,
but who tries to understand
Who wants to see the good in his fellow man.

I want to like myself but never be too proud
Admitting my mistakes with my head unbowed.

I want to lead my children
as my Mom and Dad led me,
By living Christian lives that I could clearly see.

My goal in life's not easy and I've often failed the test,
But my desire to be this kind of man
won't ever let me rest.

Some day may it be said that until the day he died,
He never was a perfect man, but God knows he tried.

Ben Hagins

FAITH IS WHAT IT TAKES

A cool, summer breeze has just blown up,
This hot and humid day.
On the horizon, storm clouds are forming.
Wonder if they will make it this way?

I hear sounds of thunder. God's clapping for us,
Letting us know Who's in control.
Well, it didn't take long for His refreshing rain
To bring relief to this body and soul.

Let me ask you one simple question,
How did this world really start?
Is the "Big Bang" your answer, or what's in the Bible?
I believe it takes faith on your part!

FOURTH OF JULY WEEKEND

It's time again to rest and renew.
When you slow down, you know it's true

That some stillness and quiet
will be a welcome retreat.
A reward for you when you find this seat

At my "Slice of Heaven" place and canyon so wide.
I feel my Lord's presence like He is by my side.

Why do we get busy with the cares of today?
Don't you know who will have the final say?

My thought right now, for you, my friend:
Aren't we blessed to be free
—on this Fourth of July weekend?

Ben Hagins

FREE SPEECH ALLEY

I learned about this place a number of years ago when our pastor, Dr. Paul Sands, at First Baptist Woodway, came to Waco.

He attended LSU in Baton Rouge in the late 70's and, during his college years, climbed atop a box in the student union area of campus known as Free Speech Alley. This area was approximately 1000 square feet of the university's 650 acres and has been the center of campus free speech.

Paul has been married to Linda since 1980 and seems to appreciate my poetic reflections of his sermons and life. He is always well prepared, and his sermons are delivered with no notes, only scripture references, and always preached with faith, courage, hope, and grace.

Thank you, Paul, for your endorsement of my book and your kind remarks. You're one of my favorites.

FREE SPEECH ALLEY

Heard about a pastor who many years ago
Spoke atop a box at LSU.
He wanted fellow Tigers to know

That there's a better way to live the rest of your life,
'Cause he had just received his Lord—Jesus Christ.

With him was Linda, his helpmate for all these years.
He was led to Ft. Worth to study with Christian peers.

Then on to Waco way, they would gladly go
To Baylor and to Truett. In his theology,
he would grow.

And develop his style of speaking from his heart.
It began at Free-Speech Alley.
That was Paul Sands's start.

Ben Hagins

FAMILY

At age 62, I had just retired because of some company decisions that caused me to want to take another direction after almost thirty years with a wonderful company that provided financial products for deserving military families. This was after my ten years on active duty in the U.S. Air Force.

Kathy and I had acquired our "Slice of Heaven" get-a-way place about ten years earlier and we were getting accustomed to this new destination. Little did we know that two years later we would be moving to Waco because of Mom's death. Most of our parental ties to Arkansas were gone, and we were ready to become Texans.

The grands were still little, but growing up quickly, and this particular morning was rather special. It just seemed "right" to pray for my family as they all grew in mind, body, and soul, and this poem just came to me, and is a favorite.

FAMILY

On my back deck at this early morning hour,
The sights and sounds of my Lord's power

Are being shown to me through thunder and light,
With a warm gentle rain, it seems so right

To just sit and give thanks for my family so dear,
My wife so faithful, and a son pretty near.

He's a grown man now and making his way
With two little ones to raise this day.

And a wife by his side as a loving helpmate,
Both committed and dedicated to Robert and Kate.

Ben Hagins

FLAG DAY

Looking out west from my back deck,
This special sunset is mine,
Yours, and everyone, who will take the time
To be still and patient, then find

The unspoken meaning from our Master and Lord,
His painting on canvas so true,
Ever changing, yet the same.
It's speaking to me, and I know it will to you

If the time is spent to watch a sunset.
Now prepare yourself for a treat.
This question of life will soon be answered
By the One who made your heart beat.

Why is the sky so big tonight?
Why is it red, white, and blue?
It is that way today on this Flag Day,
To let God pay tribute to you!

Ben Hagins

G

Ben Hagins

GOD SPEAKS

How does God speak to you? Is it through prayer, visiting with Christian friends, or faithful Bible study? It is all these ways and more.

The book of Hebrews, written by an anonymous first-century writer, who many say was Paul, is considered to be the fifth gospel. We are reminded to press on to spiritual maturity and learn from these leaders of old—Noah, Abraham, Sarah, Isaac, Jacob, Joseph, Moses, Gideon, Samson, Samuel, David, and many others.

Also, it was a most pleasant surprise when I received this note from my pastor, Paul Sands, at First Baptist Woodway, who wrote, "Dear Ben, I wanted to say thank you for sharing your poems with me. The one titled, 'God Speaks', pretty much says it all. I could have read it instead of preaching my sermon."

Because of this personal note, I consider it one of my favorites.

GOD SPEAKS

God spoke in many ways
Through prophets in ancient days,

And many times, He showed His power
That your end can come at any hour.

It is in Christ—He is the Word.
Don't make excuses that you haven't heard

This message of hope for every man,
Woman, and child. Will you take a stand?

Proclaim your faith, in what you say and do.
Make up your mind—it's up to you!

Ben Hagins

GOD PROVIDES

Up early this morning and what do I hear?
A chorus of birds making music to my ears.

The mockingbirds, sparrows, and cardinals, too.
They all came around to see what was new.

In my yard was food, for I had put out some seed.
Birds flittered and fluttered. It was a sight indeed!

The meal was prepared right below my bird home
They all took a peek, but they weren't alone.

From a distant tree, some squirrels just knew,
God provided for them, and He will do it for you.

GRACE

The word "Grace" is mentioned over 100 times in the Bible, and one of my favorite references is in Ephesians 2:1-10.

These ten verses talk about "Grace."
Through Christ, you were saved.
You were given this gift.

Not by your works,
Lest any man should boast.
Clearly, this isn't a myth.

Like these Ephesians,
You just can't say
That you haven't heard.

'Cause Paul used this word, "Grace,"
More than 100 times.
It must be an important word!

Ben Hagins

GREAT WHILE BEFORE THE DAY

I love this single verse from Mark 1:35. It speaks about Jesus, rising early in the morning, a great while before the day, finding a solidary place, and there He prayed.

This was a favorite verse of Don and Pearl Anderson, from Tyler, Texas, who in 1972, formed a nonprofit organization, Bible Teaching Resources.

They published a thick, power-packed booklet every six months with over 180 comprehensive devotionals. They also led groups to Trail West in Buena Vista, Colorado, for one-week retreats. We were fortunate to get to do this with them one summer.

Please enjoy my poetic version of a Great While Before the Day.

GREAT WHILE BEFORE THE DAY

A nice summer breeze has come my way
As I concluded my devotional time.
A great while before the day
Is a Bible study, so sublime

With teachings and thoughts, so encouraging to me,
It's lessons that all should heed.
Each day from the Word, a verse is covered,
Providing a message we all need.

Right now, I'm in Titus. Paul is writing to his friend.
Stand firm and always be strong.
Build your church on a solid foundation,
And you will never go wrong.

Ben Hagins

GO SOUTH TO THE ROAD

My friend, René Maciel, is the Missions Pastor at First Woodway Baptist in Waco, Texas. Prior to that, René invested over thirty years in education and administration with Baptist institutions, including serving as president of the Baptist General Convention of Texas. He was also a graduate and distinguished alumni from Hardin-Simmons University.

Several years ago, René preached this sermon from Acts 8:26-39 about Philip and his new friend. This Ethiopian was trying to understand this scripture from Isaiah. He asked for help and Philip delivered this message of Jesus.

René is a "doer" of the word and not a "hearer" only. He seeks others who are hungry for this Christian message and goes on trips when others would stay at home. He also leads a weekly Bible study and is a true example of a servant - leader.

Also, René can still hit that golf ball and is so generous in his golf outing invitations. He has also spoken at our Waco Links Fellowship meetings.

Thank you, René. You're one of my favorites.

GO SOUTH TO THE ROAD

Now an angel told Philip
To go south to the road
And he met an Ethiopian man.

Actually, he was a eunuch
Who was reading Isaiah
And up to his chariot, Philip ran.

He asked the official
If he understood the Scripture
The words from chapter 53

So Philip was invited
To explain these verses
About Jesus, the Savior for you and for me.

Ben Hagins

GENEROSITY

This topic of generosity is sometimes mentioned during a time of emphasis about giving. There are many biblical verses that encourage us to be generous.

As you have hopefully read in Acts 20:35—It is more blessed to give than to receive.

Here are ten additional references to generosity:
1. Malachi 3:10 (Tithe)
2. Psalms 112:5 (Justice)
3. Proverbs 11:24-25 (Prosper)
4. Proverbs 22:9 (Blessed)
5. Matthew 6:1-4 (Not to be seen)
6. Matthew 6:21 (Treasure and heart)
7. Luke 6:38 (Good measure)
8. Luke 21:1-4 (Widow's mite)
9. 2 Corinthians 9:6-8 (Sparingly and bountifully)
10. 1 Timothy 6:17-18 (Not haughty)

This topic from Luke 20:9-21:38, preached by my pastor, Dr. Paul Sands, inspired me to write this poem. I trust it will help you to become more generous.

GENEROSITY

This story in Luke concerns the authority of Jesus,
And relates to me and you.

Seems this owner of a vineyard,
about settling his estate,
Said this, "What shall I do?"

An example was given using a Roman coin.
And just what should I owe to who?

Some to Caesar, some to God,
was the answer from Jesus.
To the Sadducees, this wasn't new.

You see, this message of generosity is clear.
It's all about the topic of greed.

Just watch your heart,
for in giving, you have freedom.
Just give as your Lord leads.

Ben Hagins

GIL STRICKLIN

Well done, good and faithful servant—was the verse in his obituary from Matthew 25:23 that describes my friend, Gil Stricklin, who died one day shy of his eighty-ninth birthday, on September 10, 2023.

I knew him because of his son, Art Stricklin, prolific golf writer and CFO—Chief Fun Officer—of the Art of Travel, a golfing travel business.

Sitting close to him at many Baylor football games, Gil was always there with a smile and a "how goes it" greeting.

The following poem was written after Gil preached his three-part sermon from Romans 12 on how to serve the Lord. We were worshipping in a small country church near our Slice of Heaven on Lake Whitney.

This poem is one of my favorites, and I hope you practice these principles.

GIL STRICKLIN

What a scripture to remember,
From Romans, chapter 12, verse 11 is the one.

There are three parts to this verse.
Let's learn them right now.
After you've read them, you're not quite done.

The first lesson is not to be lazy, or to fall into a rut.
Some versions say, don't lose your zeal.

The second part: Keep your spiritual fervor.
Know that this message is real.

Finally, the third admonition:
Serve the Lord is the point!
If you do, your reward is heaven.

Now you have it, summed up so simply.
Go live it out—Romans 12:11.

Ben Hagins

H

HOW I BEGIN MY DAY

I trust you have a "quiet time" during your day. Mine is early morning, usually before Kathy wakes up.

I was never an early riser years ago, but since retirement, this is a special time for me, especially at our "Slice of Heaven" at White Bluff.

That's what I named our place, that we were fortunate to build in July 1998. And the first poem I wrote on my back deck was that very night we moved into this home. It's on page eleven of my first book, Slice of Heaven.

And, of course, it's one of my favorites.

HOW I BEGIN MY DAY

God made the birds
On creation's fifth day.

It's the only sound I'm hearing
As I meditate and pray.

These early morning times
Mean so much to me.

I just love these sounds of silence
Interrupted by my birds so free.

They sing and gather for their babies.
Can you picture this setting I'm in?

It's pretty special and I hope you know
This is a fantastic way for my day to begin.

Ben Hagins

HIS HANDIWORK

The Psalms are songs of praise, worship, thankfulness, repentance, and poems. All 150 chapters convey a variety of feelings, emotions, attitudes, and interests.

The verses of Psalms 8:3-6 are some of my favorites. Just look up to the heavens, especially on a clear night, and you will see about 3000 stars, planets, and usually our moon.

Does this not make you mindful of Him? We are given dominion over the works of His hand and put all things under His feet.

This chapter is a hymn of praise and is spoken entirely to God. It emphasizes His sovereignty and majesty.

HIS HANDIWORK

On my back deck this morning,
I was treated to a show
Like a 4th of July display.

From west to east.
The sky lit up.
My Lord showed his power today.

Had a gentle spring breeze,
Then the winds blew in
With lightning, then thunder, it came.

This storm was predicted
And right on cue,
The heavens opened with rain.

His Majesty from above
Cannot happen by chance.
Why can't science and faith agree?

It's written in Psalms
For all to read
And His handiwork for all to see!

Ben Hagins

HUFFY—A TRIBUTE

My friend Jim Huffhines died in October of 2017. This was my letter to his wife Judy.

Judy, I'm sitting on my back deck early this Sunday morning at White Bluff looking at the lake, the cedars, the bird house, and the birds. Huffy was the one who inspired me to—Just Do It—when I thought up a project for our "Slice of Heaven."

- I could never have cleared those cedars without Huffy's help.
- I could never have erected that birdhouse without Huffy's help.
- I could never have finished any projects without Huffy's help.
- He always said—Why Not Now? I even wrote a poem with this title.

I cherish my many golf games with Huffy when stopping at Hideaway on our trips. And I appreciated their coming and giving me comfort when my mom died in Fordyce, Arkansas, in March of 2008.

These thoughts and the following poem are inadequate but given in love about Huffy's time in our lives. We love you both.

HUFFY—A TRIBUTE

I had a good friend who's not here anymore.
A stalwart man of God was he.
I met him years ago when we visited his church.
After the service, he came over to see

Just who we were and where we were from.
His first impression was so sincere.
We were attracted to his genuine friendship.
He was happy that we were here.

To worship with him at his small country church,
And experience the joy it would give.
And then to know Judy, his true help-mate.
They really know how to live.

Ben Hagins

THE HIKE

Five couples got together—25-28 February 2019.

Ben and Kathy Hagins, Don and Charlotte Heathcott, Benny and Sherri Cherry, Clint and Linda Ferguson, and Warren and Edie Guffin.

After the hike, Baylor won over Texas in basketball— 84-83 in overtime.

Five hearty couples had a hike to remember,
At least from my point of view,
On a mild and cloudy day in February '19.
For several of us, this was new.

Took over two hours to make this trek
Down and up my canyon out back.
We blazed this trail that I've done many times.
Believe it, 'cause it's a fact.

HOMECOMING WEEKEND

It's reunion time for all our friends,
Alumni from far and near.
Come together to visit and tell some stories,
And maybe even shed a tear

For those not here or ill of health.
Our bodies just aren't the same
As it was yesteryear when we performed
On fields of valor and fame.

To one and all, Baylor welcomes you back,
And this is the message they send—
Stay united in faith, vision, and hope,
As you fellowship on Homecoming Weekend.

HONEY, YOU'RE RIGHT AGAIN

Now this is for all you wise people who are reading these words.

Take heart, as this reminder is for—you!

Give all the credit to your honey. And know this, it is not just you that has done everything for your family. If you forget this, you will probably reap the whirlwind. Believe me, many times, I've had to say, "I'm sorry."

In fact, there are four things all men should know, and I've used this in many of our Waco Links Fellowship meetings.

> 1—I was wrong.
> 2—I'm so sorry.
> 3—Please forgive me.
> 4—I love you.

HONEY, YOU'RE RIGHT AGAIN

It happened again, just the other day.
I thought my plans were figured out.
The intentions that I had; they went awry.
Some things I just didn't think about.

'Cause when I failed to consult my honey,
I just did not have all the facts.
Had done it again, a too familiar mistake.
I should respond instead of react.

And listen to her with all her wisdom.
This principle I just must proclaim,
Be honest with yourself and say these words,
"Honey, you're right again."

Ben Hagins

Ben Hagins

I LIKE LOOKING AT YOU

On Mother's Day, 13 May 2012, my grandgirl, Kate Hagins, age 5, was staying with us for an overnight visit. The next morning, Kate surprised me with this comment, which I really liked!

What a day I had with my little girl.
Each day I see her makes me glad.

She crawled up in my bed and cuddled with me,
Looked right into my eyes at her granddad.

She called me something that makes me happy,
A name that is special to Kate.

'Cause the way she is and what she does,
Seems to me, to be first-rate.

She kinda turned over and stared at me.
What was she going to do?

To my surprise, she said to me—
"Big Pardner—I like looking at you!"

IT'S NEVER TOO LATE

I'm sure you've heard this saying before,
And you know it's true.
For when life deals you a losing hand,
Just know that you're not through.

There's always light at the end of the tunnel,
And the sun will shine again.
But if you quit and never give your best,
Then I'm not so sure you can

Complete the jobs you've planned to do.
Just finish what you started, then see
The smile on your face when "well done" is said.
Then all those around you will agree

That it's just a test to really find out
If persistence and work is your fate.
Just buckle down to the task ahead,
And remember—It's never too late!

Ben Hagins

I HAVE NO IDEA

One of my best friends, Benny Cherry, is always saying these four words. Our friendship dates to our college days over fifty years ago.

We both came from small hometowns, joined the same fraternity, and started our quest for the future.

We both met beautiful young ladies, played golf together, and still do.

We go to church together, and many times, have breakfast together.

And Benny is trying to get better with his golf game. Sometimes when he asks why he isn't better, I also use these four words.

I HAVE NO IDEA

A really good friend of mine
has a saying that's hard to forget.
If I ask him something he doesn't know,
this four-word phrase is all I get.

It goes like this, "I have no idea."
It's just as simple as that.
Now why doesn't he know
easy questions that I ask?

Guess he doesn't get the word
or look on the internet,
At least he keeps his cool
and doesn't get upset.

He doesn't read the paper
or even answer the phone.
Seems he's always driving somewhere
or walking all alone.

Now he is a great friend,
and I love him like a brother,
But trying to discuss what's happening,
I might need to find another.

Ben Hagins

INDEPENDENCE DAY THOUGHTS

This day we celebrate the 4th of July
To enjoy our freedoms, but let me ask why

Did so many go before us
to serve the country they love
To protect our liberties
so we can worship the One above?

Who gives us a choice to pursue any quest,
With a mission and a goal of having happiness?

Now the privileges we have
Mean we can't do just anything.

Put your God first, and others second.
You'll be happy when freedom rings!

IT'S UP TO YOU

Up early this morning before the sun comes up,
Something special about this time of the day.
A cool summer breeze has come my way,
Guess it's time that I should pray

And thank my Lord for the blessings I have.
Thoughts of family are flooding my soul.
These last few months have caused some problems,
No doubt, we're not in control.

Put your trust and faith in your Lord and Master.
It's the real thing you really can do
And make some plans to get organized.
These decisions are truly up to you!

Note: I wrote this several years ago when our world
suffered with an unknown virus affecting millions.
How did the pandemic affect you?

Ben Hagins

J&K

JERRY AND CANDY

Jerry and Candy Wagner came into my life over twenty years ago, when I needed them most. I was working in the North Little Rock office, and somewhat burned out.

I was doing okay in my career but needed a boost. They were a breath of fresh air and provided just that encouragement. As the new District Agent, Jerry and I became good friends. He was a retired Army Colonel and former Apache helicopter pilot. Candy was the daughter of Vaughn Monroe, who wrote the song "Ghost Riders in the Sky," one of my favorites.

For several years, we had a great time with the company, as production was up. But then Jerry and Candy moved on. They were transferred to another district in California, but we remained close.

After their retirement, they moved to the Scottsdale, Arizona, area. But after a few years and tears, Jerry got sick and passed away in April of 2017.

I wrote the following poem for his epitaph.

JERRY AND CANDY

Some changes were needed a long time ago.
Our Little Rock district had no get up and go.
PC was lagging and morale was somewhat low.
I told this to region, as our office wanted to know

What was going to happen? Bring a new guy to lead?
At first, they didn't listen, but I continued to plead
And make a case for a leader to come fill this need.
Action was taken and all finally agreed.

So, in came Jerry, our new DA,
along with Candy as his AA.
Things immediately improved and all was okay.
Both came in early, nearly stayed all day,
Dedicated they were —to USPA and IRA.

I'll never forget what you both mean to me.
Jerry was the perfect example. You see,
His friendship and leadership—those were the key.
He was special to this agent, and all advisers agree.

Abbreviations:
PC—Production Credit
DA —District Agent
AA —Administrative Assistant
USPA and IRA —United Services Planning Association and
Independent Research Agency, now called First Command

Ben Hagins

JOHNNY CASH

Johnny Cash grew up near my hometown of Fordyce, Arkansas. His background was in country music as a singer-songwriter, and he wrote over 1000 songs in his career.

His themes contained sorrow, drugs, redemption and salvation. His genre-spanning music included country, rock'n'roll, folk, and gospel. His concerts were very popular, especially the free ones he performed at prisons.

His image grew as he wore outfits in all black and was known as the "Man in Black." Several years ago, I read his book by Greg Laurie, a southern California evangelist who was instrumental in producing the movie, "The Jesus Revolution."

The following poem's theme is about—darkness to light, titled Johnny Cash, The Redemption of an American Icon.

JOHNNY CASH

We all face a fork
On the road of life.
Which one will you take?
Is it darkness or the light?

That "Man in Black"
Named Johnny Cash,
Between 1932-2003,
That time is called the dash.

And what happens then,
At times was the worst?
As a sinner and a saint,
He quoted scripture and verse.

He sang, "Ring of Fire"
And, "I Walk the Line."
Because of alcohol and drugs,
He crossed it many times.

He even became a minister
With a theology degree, in fact.
This true American icon,
Johnny Cash,
"The Man in Black."

JIMMY DORRELL
AND MISSION WACO

Jimmy went to Baylor about the same time I did. I did not know him then, but have come to admire his work, along with his wife Janet, with the poor and marginalized in Waco, Texas, and internationally.

His passion for the poor and for mobilizing the middle class to become involved became the organization he founded in 1978—Mission Waco.

In the early 90s, Jimmy formed—Church Under the Bridge, just beside Baylor campus, which feeds and ministers to thousands of the marginalized in Waco.

About ten years ago, Jimmy fed over 500 souls on "9/11" and encouraged all to embrace the Mission Waco vision.

Jimmy, my friend, is one of my favorites.

JIMMY DORRELL
AND MISSION WACO

500 strong went to breakfast this day.
"9/11" was the date, to help make a way

In a part of this city that's down and out.
Just looking for a hand and not a handout.

Sure, they've had trouble. Judging isn't right.
How to respond is the question
to help these folks fight

For a better way of life
with some food on their tables.
They'll be better prepared and then be able

To give back to this city and this fact I know—
We're all better off—
thanks to Jimmy and Mission Waco!

Ben Hagins

KATE'S 17TH

Our granddaughter is so special to me and inspired this poem as one of her gifts for her 17th birthday.

Your day is here,
One to always remember,
You're now a beautiful young lady.
So glad you're not a big spender.

You've developed, now as a Senior,
I trust, of Proverbs 31 fame.
And now, on your 17th,
Let all the world proclaim

That here comes Kate Hagins,
One to always admire.
Hold your head up high,
And aspire to always inspire.

L&M

Ben Hagins

LOVE—ALL THAT MATTERS

My good friend, Clint Ferguson, from Eastland, Texas, had been planning to compose a musical CD with many of his favorite hymns for quite some time.

He ran into many roadblocks for several years, but finally persisted and produced this work, recorded in his church. He is now passing his vocal and musical talents down to his family.

My fraternity brother, banker, and cattlemen friend has now completed his musical production, titled— "All That Matters is Love," inspired by Scripture passages from Matthew 22:37-39, some of my favorite verses.

LOVE—ALL THAT MATTERS

I just heard a heavenly song,
by an 'ole banker and cattlemen friend.
He is working on a musical CD.

If you will slow down for a minute, it will speak to you
Just like it did to me.

The story is old, taken from Matthew,
The passage from chapter 22.

Yes, it's about love. It's the greatest commandment,
And you know it's true.

So, look it up and be inspired
By these verses from above.

Oh, you ask what's the title?
Well, here it is, the song—
"All that matters is how we love."

Ben Hagins

LIZ IS AN "IS"

Liz Hagins, our daughter-in-law, is a teacher. She has been doing this a very long time, over fifteen years, since she and Trey were married after their Baylor days.

A few years ago, because of Liz's dedication to her profession, she was awarded the position at Midway Middle School of "Instructional Specialist," or I put it—an "IS."

I always joke around with Liz that I will come to school and teach for her one day and she always says, "They will eat you up and spit you out."

I'm very proud of Liz and what she does, especially taking care of our son, Trey, and the grands.

"Sic 'em" Liz —one of my favorites.

LIZ IS AN "IS"

My daughter-in-law, Liz,
Is now an "IS"—
"Instructional Specialist," that is.

A former "Teacher of the Year,"
She simply is the best,
Always available and near.

Teaching, training, and guiding others,
Her reputation is beyond reproach.
Meet her and you will discover

Her talents, concerns, and attitude.
She will lead and inspire all to learn,
Always with the trait of gratitude.

So, for all you teachers in the "biz,"
Do you need a little help,
From someone who is an "IS?"

Ben Hagins

MEMORIAL DAY TRIBUTE

Over one million lives were lost in these three wars—
Civil War, World War One, and World War Two. And
many more lives were lost in these wars—
Revolutionary, Korean, Vietnam, and Persian Gulf.

We celebrate these military patriots on this historical
day—Memorial Day, the last Monday in May, one of
my favorite days!

You've heard this before, but I will say it again—
Freedom isn't free!

Take a moment and honor those who wore the
uniform and gave their all. And please join me as we
say a prayer for everything that they did for us!

MEMORIAL DAY TRIBUTE

It's that time again to rest and review
What this day means, you know it's true.

Some play and fun will be a welcome retreat,
A reward for you when you find a seat

At a nearby pool, golf course, or lake.
Thank our Lord and Provider
for this freedom to partake!

Why do we get busy with the problems of today?
Don't you know who will have the final say?

My thought right now for you, my friend,
Is to remember our military
on this Memorial Day weekend!

MEN'S FRATERNITY

My friend, Mike Toby, of First Baptist Woodway, pastored for thirty-five years. His church was known as a "Lighthouse"—a beacon for spreading God's word. Mike passed away in December of 2012. I was so fortunate to have known him and to have learned from him.

After Kathy and I moved to Waco, I joined a group called Men's Fraternity, led by Mike. I attended thanks to an invitation from Darryl Lehnus, the "commish" of our golf group.

This organization was started by Robert Lewis, pastor of Fellowship Baptist, in Little Rock, Arkansas, in 1990. It covered four principles of living:

1. Reject Passivity
2. Accept Responsibility
3. Lead Courageously
4. Expect God's Reward

I was also fortunate to have played one of the last rounds of golf with Mike Toby. After we finished, he said, "Gentlemen, I have sure enjoyed today, but I must get back to the church office." Mike could've easily taken that afternoon off, but he didn't.

MEN'S FRATERNITY

Just finished reviewing session twenty-one,
Four more to go, but I'm not done.

For today I'm reminded just what I should do,
You know it will help both me and you.

These twenty-five ways are your outline for life.
You'll be a better husband,
and you'll have a better wife.

Now throughout this year just work your plan.
A servant-leader you'll become,
and a maximum man.

But if you don't agree with men's fraternity,
Then don't change a thing as you approach eternity.

Ben Hagins

MADDI—OUR DOG

Kathy and I adopted Maddi on 9 August 2016. What a joy she has been for us, despite those "little dog" accidents. Everyone at Fuzzy Friends was so helpful and accommodating, and the adoption process went smoothly. We look forward to many more years with our "family member," and encourage you to go see for yourselves what Fuzzy Friends has to offer.

It's early August of 2016. It was a hot and humid day.
We visited Fuzzy Friends to see what they had to say

About acquiring a pet to be part of our family,
Much like we have had before.

They showed us some dogs who needed a home.
But we asked if they had some more.

Of course they did, because we wanted a match
And a companion for Kathy and Ben.

A few days later we got the call—
Maddi was ours, and we both said—Amen!

MADDI—OUR "NABER"

Our special "naber" has all grown up.
What a fine young lady she is.
Her name is Maddi from the Mosler fam
And she knows that she is His

To serve one another as she has done for us,
Taking care of our grand-girl Kate.
Now back home starting college year two,
There's plenty of time for that mate,

How lucky he will be if he does what Maddi does
Giving to others that are in need.
We pray for you always and thank you again
You'll come back—is that agreed?

Note: Madison "Maddi" Mosler flew to Waco and helped with the grand kiddos in July of 2012, while Trey and Liz went on a trip. Now she is engaged and will tie the knot in September 2024. Oh yes, Maddi wrote us a note and said we were the best "naber fam" she ever had.

Ben Hagins

N&O

Ben Hagins

NAVY SEALS

This poem appeared in our local paper, and was read on the radio, WBAP in Dallas, one of my favorite stations. Even now, memories of this event still come to mind as I vividly remember touring the World Trade Center.

After the horrific event on 9/11/01, our Navy Seals were sent on another mission, about ten years later, to eliminate Osama bin Laden, accused of being the mastermind of the 9/11 attacks.

NAVY SEALS

Two dozen men called Navy seals did
what they were trained to do.
This special unit won't get any credit,
for they exist for me and for you.

All highly trained and greatly underpaid,
they put their lives on the line.
They have done it before, will do it again,
and follow their orders every time.

For that's the way the military is.
Millions have fought for our freedom before
On the sea, in the air, and on foreign lands.
We just keep asking for more.

Now we owe all of them a respectful salute,
for their sacrifices are very real.
At this opportune time, they made history.
Thanks for your service, you brave Navy Seals!

Ben Hagins

9-11-2001

Even now, over twenty years after their destruction, the World Trade Center and those two buildings are ever present to me.

Four airplanes departed the East Coast fully loaded with fuel, all bound for the West Coast with nineteen hijackers aboard. I vividly remember being in my office and watching those tragedies unfold before my eyes.

And then, after three planes reached their fateful destinations, the fourth was prevented from completing their destruction by passengers on United Flight 93, led by Todd Beamer. His words—"Let's Roll"—was their call to duty, and I read every word of his wife Lisa's book by that title.

Another narrative of this event is covered on page eighty-eight in my first book, Slice of Heaven. This story is one that I will never forget!

9-11-2001

Where were you on that fateful day
over twenty years ago?
How could this tragedy happen to a city so large
by a foreign enemy and foe?

Just what do they believe and think, and who leads a
multitude this way?
Unanswered questions from centuries past, resulted
in terror that day.

We continue to mourn those 3000 lives, and
thousands more military souls.
They have fought and died, and gave their all, to
preserve our liberties and goals

Of freedom for you, your sons and daughters, any life
they choose to pursue.
With guidance from our Lord above, can it be done?
It just might depend on you!

Ben Hagins

NATIONAL DAY OF PRAYER

The first Thursday in May
Is a very special day.
Way back in 1863,
Honest Abe wanted all to agree

To set aside some time for prayer,
To honor our fallen and be aware
Of the freedoms belonging to us,
And to know —In God We Trust.

Then Truman in 1952,
Made it official for me and you.
He established a certain day —
It's now the first Thursday in May.

OG MANDINO

Og Mandino, 1923-1996, was an American author and speaker, having written over twenty books on the philosophy of success and motivation. Instead of going to college, Og became a military officer as a bombardier with Jimmy Stewart during World War II. After the war, he became an insurance salesman but fought the demons of alcohol and even thoughts of suicide. But through his readings of the Bible and positive mental attitude books, Og turned his life around and chose to help others through his writings.

One of his most famous books was <u>The Greatest Miracle in the World</u>.

His four laws of happiness and success are contained in this book:
1—Count your Blessings
2—Proclaim your Rarity
3—Go another Mile
4—Use Wisely your Power of Choice

As you probably know, this book is one of my favorites.

Ben Hagins

OG MANDINO

Read his book, <u>The Greatest Miracle in the World</u>,
written in 1975.
Og is an inspirational author.
His writings make you come alive.

With words so true and easy to read,
his summary passes the test.
Follow these four laws, and you'll think about
happiness and success.

#1
Like the teachings by Jesus on a hill,
called the Sermon on the Mount,
Take an inventory of the gifts—mind and body
Your blessings count.

#2
Is unique, like no other, you are made.
No one has ever been the same.
You are quite worthy, a special creation
Always your rarity proclaim.

#3
Practical advice for all seasons:
You can always do more with a smile,
Most won't recognize that it's not always easy to
Go that extra mile.

#4
For your own success, listen to that still, small voice.
Live life to the fullest. Make every day count and
Use wisely your power of choice.

Ben Hagins

P

Ben Hagins

PLAN ON IT

After my ten years in the U.S. Air Force, I joined First Command Financial Planning, an organization that serves military families as an advisor.

The company had an annual international sales meeting. Just before I retired, the meeting was scheduled in Hawaii, and I got to take my entire family with me.

Each year we have a company motto, and this year was no different. The motto was short and sweet, and I liked it. It was:

Plan On It.

PLAN ON IT

We are now back home. First Command has met
Another year, we've completed the tasks.
Some ups, some downs, many changes were made
For our clients. We've done what they asked.

To deliver what we promised, many claims were paid
For those who gave the ultimate price.
Our Maker only knows the time each has left
To provide suitable advice.

For the mission has not changed,
but our market is more.
Many products are varied and new.
We must respond to the needs we see,
And make good what we promise to do

To help each family both dream and set goals,
To desire to be financially fit.
There is but one way. We all know it's true.
The answer, three words:
Plan On It!

Ben Hagins

PROVERBS 31 WIFE

The second part of Chapter thirty-one describes a wife of noble character—my wife.

Proverbs is a wonderful book, full of heavenly wisdom and practical advice. It has thirty-one chapters, and a good goal is to read and heed one chapter a day for a month.

I pray you'll learn from these verses and poem about my Proverbs 31 wife.

And, of course, it's one of my favorites.

PROVERBS 31 WIFE

Who can find a good wife now?
Who can find one more precious than gold?
Well, let me tell you of one lucky fellow.
This he promised—to have and to hold.

All my days of working for others
Were because she did nothing but good.
She kept the home fires burning warm,
Just like you knew she would.

She opens her heart to those in trouble.
Her hand reaches to those in need.
Her soft, sweet voice is filled with wisdom,
Always giving to others, a kind deed.

Inner strength and beauty are always present,
No idleness in her ways.
She loves her Lord and praises Him.
For her, my love is pledged, all my days!

Ben Hagins

PRACTICAL LIVING

Jeff Watters, my friend from Links Players International, was our guest speaker at our end of the year Waco Links Fellowship meeting, in November 2023.

Our guests were three golf teams from Midway High, McLennan Community College, and Baylor University. They totaled about twenty-five young men and three coaches—Keith Mikeska, Vince Clark, and Mike McGraw. Along with our Links regulars, we filled the room at Ridgewood Country Club on a rainy November evening.

Jeff did something that I think was truly amazing. He quoted the entire book of James, all five chapters—108 verses. Jeff also spoke about his Bucket Ministry in Africa with a demonstration of turning dirty water into safe, drinkable water with a filter device.

What a story and remarkable program we had that night. Now if you don't have time to read one of my favorite books in the Bible, the book of James, consider studying these nine verses: James 1:19-27. They will sum up Practical Living.

PRACTICAL LIVING

You have heard this before, but I will tell you again.
I want you to be quick to hear,

Slow to speak, and slow to anger.
Keep these written words very near.

Be a doer of the word, and not just hear it.
Take action when you know it's true.

Your religion will be pure,
when you help those in need.
The only one to do this is you.

There you have it, James summed it up for all.
These truths will stand the test.

Don't fool yourself, just obey these words.
They are practical living at its best.

POWER

Heard a sermon the other day
Just open to Acts 1:8, and it will say,

Do you want power of the Spirit available for you?
Do you believe this question to be true?

This courage, this boldness, these blessings are real.
Just act and ask, it will be revealed.

You say you can't do it; you may not have tried.
I say try this,
"Just do it, believe, and decide!"

PSALMS 23—IN MY OWN WORDS

My Lord, like a shepherd, is all I want.
He leads and guides my soul.
When I follow him down the right path,
Then my life will completely be whole.

I will never be afraid of death's dark valley
No evil will I ever have to fear
For He promises to be ever with me.
My great Comforter is always near.

He fills my cup to overflowing
My enemies do I fight? No, never.
Just goodness and mercy are my rewards,
To dwell eternally in His house forever!

Note: I wrote this Psalm in my own words and used it at my mom's funeral. It's a comforting chapter, and I hope you like this version.

Ben Hagins

PSALM 46—IN MY OWN WORDS

Have you read the eleven verses in this chapter? I just did—again. This chapter is known as the "protection" Psalm. The words tell us of the Lord's power and majesty—His omnipotence!

The great hymn, "A Mighty Fortress is our God," was written and composed by Martin Luther (1483-1546) after being inspired by Psalms 46. Look it up, the words and music, and you also will be inspired.

I particularly like those two words—"Be Still." I have led a group—Waco Links Fellowship, for over ten years. We have "God and golf" meetings with special guests, and a year-end meeting with outstanding speakers in November with the golf teams and coaches from Baylor University, McLennan Community College, and Midway High School.

"Be Still" for a golfer, means to keep your head still while putting. Moving the head is a common fault. I even made that saying into a sign, suitable for framing, that I give to special friends of Links Fellowship. I am also pleased that a few years ago, we even started a chapter at White Bluff in Whitney, Texas, which has been well received.

PSALM 46—IN MY OWN WORDS

Our God is our refuge and our strength
A very present help in trouble.
Why don't we, as a nation, turn to him
Amidst all the terror and rubble?

Why don't we seek Him by day and night?
Will He answer our prayers of need?
It makes me cynical to look all around
When I see a world full of greed.

But this I know, if you believe the Word,
He promises peace when you do.
If you cast your burdens on the Lord,
His sustenance will be granted to you.

And one final promise.
This chapter tells us so.
"A mighty fortress is our Lord,
For I am God. Be still and know!"

Ben Hagins

PLAY

About ten years ago, my grandson, Robert Hagins, was in the fourth grade at South Bosque Elementary School in Waco, Texas. After his day, I always liked it when he would come over to our home, as we lived just behind the school. I usually would ask him something about his day and what he studied and learned.

Well, this day was an exception. He didn't want to talk about it. But I wanted to know more, and I continued to probe his little mind.

Very quickly, Robert stopped and put his hands on his hips and said, "Big Pardner, don't you understand? I just want to play!"

And this poem memorialized the moment.

PLAY

The funniest thing happened today,

What my grandson Robert said to me.

I had asked him what he learned in school,

But he wasn't ready for this talk, you see.

He was tired of class and teacher stuff,

Didn't want to discuss his day.

But as I pressed for more info,

Robert said to me, "I just want to play!"

Ben Hagins

THE PROMISE

I'm gazing at my first winter's fire
And this is what I see.
Each burning log is different,
Just like you and me.

My fire gives warmth and comfort
And, for this, I feel secure.
'Cause I'm thinking of my family
And this I'm very sure.

For them, here's a promise;
In Christ, there's abundant life.
Now it's time to send up prayers
For my children and my wife.

Q&R

Ben Hagins

QUIET TIME

Up early this morning, well before sunrise.
It's so peaceful and quite sublime.

Heard a sermon yesterday from a TV pastor
About finding a place for my quiet time.

I have done that and have, for many years.
That's how I want to start my day.

I pray and listen to that still, small voice.
Just don't think there is a better way

To give my thanks to my God, for family,
And for friends who stick close, too.

Now what is your place for your daily devotional?
Isn't some quiet time what you're led to do?

QUESTIONS ARE THE ANSWERS

The answers to your problems,
If you haven't heard,
Aren't they in the Good Book—
God's Holy Word?

Ben Hagins

RED SKY AT NIGHT

There is an old saying
That goes this way.
"Red sky at night is sailor's delight."
Do you think you'll look up today?

It's in red letters, as Jesus said
In Matthew 16, verse two,
It applies to everyone,
And that means—YOU.

See for yourselves
What the heavens will teach.
Words from the Bible,
Now, won't that preach?

RAIN

After previous summers of unbearable high temperatures, recently we've experienced extended weeks of light rain, hard rain, and downpours of rain. Much like one of my favorite poems, "Trees," by Joyce Kilmer, I thought I would write my poem about rain that was similar.

I think that I will never hear
Raindrops so pleasing to my ear,
As a rain that falls on my tin roof.
Reminds me of that heavenly proof,

That God provides both day and night,
Trusting Him to make everything right.
A rain that comes at different times,
And when it does, is so sublime.

It provides for plants, crops, and trees,
Giving new life that all may see
The wonder and beauty, I can't explain,
The power of God and His refreshing rain.

Ben Hagins

REJECTION

Shortly after I joined the Christian Writers Workshop, I was given an assignment to write about a time my work was critiqued and eventually rejected.

All writers, I believe, have had this experience in some form or another. In fact, these five authors had been rejected before their work was later published: Ernest Hemingway, John Grisham, Rudyard Kipling, Stephen King, and Agatha Christie.

It has been said that being rejected can be beneficial. For example, when a publisher rejects your story or poem, it doesn't mean it wasn't good. It just means that publication didn't think its readers needed it at that time.

So, take heart, dear author. Write because you want to, and not for the money.

It's one of my favorite things to do.

REJECTION

I always thought my story was pretty good.
Never imagined folks didn't think I could

Write a poem they didn't like.
My oh my, what a sight!

When I got my story rejected, it was pretty bad.
Had to admit, that made me kinda sad.

Almost gave up, but this I know.
Keep writing from your heart,
you'll reap what you sow!

Ben Hagins

ROMANS 12—IN MY OWN WORDS

1. Listen friends, because God wants us to, take care of your bodies. You are very special, made by your God whom you should worship.

2. Don't let this world get the best of you, but let your mind, because of God, control you. Be in control of your mind and you will then be in the will of God, which is what we know as perfect.

3. Remember, don't think of yourself to be more important than anyone else, but think clearly as God gives you talents to use.

4. We are one church body, but each of us has a significant function.

5. Even though we are individuals, we are one church body.

6. Our talents are unique and different. Some can predict the future.

7. Some serve others, and others can teach.

8. Others give freely and cheerfully of their possessions and time.

9. Your love must be real. Hate evil and hold on to good.

10. Love one another completely and respect your fellow man.

11. Serve the Lord with an enthusiastic spirit and do not be lazy.

12. Never lose hope, but be patient, even with your trials, and pray regularly.

13. Give to those in need and practice friendship.

14. Love those who use you, and do not be mad at them.

15. Be happy with those who are happy, and cry with those who cry.

16. Live with your neighbors in a compatible way, don't think of yourself in a conceited way, and associate also with the poor.

17. Do not get back at people.

18. Live peaceably with your neighbors.

19. Let God take care of situations at the correct time. You don't need to do this.

20. If your neighbor is hungry, feed him. If thirsty, give him drink. They usually will not understand your kindness.

21. Your good actions will and can overcome evil things.

REFLECTIONS

Tragedy has always been with us and probably always will be. Do you remember these ten horrible events?

- Feb 1993—Waco – Branch Davidians
- Apr 1995—Oklahoma City – Murrah Building bombing
- Apr 1999—Denver – Columbine High School shootings
- Sep 2001—New York – 9/11 World Trade Center
- Apr 2007—Virgina – college shootings
- Nov 2009—Texas – Fort Hood shootings
- Dec 2012—Connecticut – Sandy Hook Elementary shootings
- Apr 2013—Boston – Marathon bombing
- Jun 2015—South Carolina – church shootings
- Feb 2020—China and USA – Coronavirus

Many times, I rank a book, sermon, golf course, or some event on a scale of one to ten, with one being no good and ten being the best. Obviously, the above events are all ranked "one" in terms of death and tragedy.

One such terrible event happened to my dad, Charlie Hagins. Just prior to his retirement, at age sixty-three, he was shot and killed in his office by a deranged mill worker. At that time, there was no security. And though my dad lost his life, he saved many, because of his immediate confrontation with his assailant. The police were called, and the shooter was killed because of their quick response.

This event altered my life as I separated from the U.S. Air Force and started a new career in the financial services area, and also cared for my mom, Lucie Hagins.

I do believe that one day, the answers to my questions concerning my dad's death will be answered. This is my hope and prayer as I make these poetic reflections.

Ben Hagins

REFLECTIONS

Let's not forget, as the new year begins,
a time for reflection and thanks.
Family and friends, what a blessing they've been,
here's how last year ranks.

On a one to ten scale, it's about a seven,
which is not bad in this man's book.
But that's not true all around the world.
Let's just take a good look.

There is loss of lives, wars overseas,
and shootings that are hard to believe.
By the grace of God, there could go I.
Allow me this time to grieve.

"Move on" is my charge. Don't dwell on the past.
Be the best I can be this day!
I'm so thankful my family is well.
"Blessed" is what I would say.

These last twelve months, these thoughts I make,
as I reflect on this past year.
Most grateful to God, who gave it all.
I am happy, but humbly shed a tear.

S

Ben Hagins

STAR SPANGLED BANNER

Our National Anthem—the Star-Spangled Banner is a poem written by Francis Scott Key in1814, as he witnessed the bombing of Fort McHenry. Key was inspired by the large U.S. flag with only fifteen stars and stripes, still flying after the battle.

This song has four stanzas, but only the first is sung today. In the fourth verse are these words, "And this be our motto—In God is Our Trust."

My grandson, Robert, age eight, came to our home after his second-grade class. I once again asked him what he learned that day. To my surprise, he said that this song was taught to him in his music class, and he proceeded to sing for me—The Star-Spangled Banner.

How proud I was as I immediately jotted down my notes and composed one of my favorite poems and this story.

STAR-SPANGLED BANNER

I had a real treat just the other day
When my grandson sang to me.
A patriotic song that makes me so proud,
It starts with—O say, can you see?

He told me about the Battle of 1812,
And some facts about Francis Scott Key.
How he stayed up all night,
and at dawn, saw our flag,
Then authored this poem of liberty.

And how he acknowledged our Power from above.
In God, we should put our trust ,
O'er the land of the free and the home of the brave,
Fighting for a cause that is just.

I'm reflecting on our past 200 plus years,
Hearing Robert in his childlike manner,
Sing a story so true about our freedom,
Reciting the words of the Star Spangled Banner.

Ben Hagins

SPECIAL PLACE

Actually, I have several special places at our "Slice of Heaven" get-a-way.

My back decks, lower and upper, are wonderful places, overlooking my canyon and seeing the lake out west and those glorious sunsets. They give me a sense of peace and tranquility in this crazy world. Yes, I want to know what's going on, but when I pause for my "quiet-time," my thoughts always come back to here.

I also have two meditation areas down a path not very far. My benches there are named—"Turkey Buzzard Lookout" and "Eagle Eye Point."

And another special place is my firepit, just a few yards away. I built this myself with a shovel, hoe, and rock-bar years ago. Two comfortable Adirondack chairs await us, and on those starlit nights, when the weather is perfect, there's nothing much better than that.

SPECIAL PLACE

I always look forward to each and every morning
When I visit my special place.
On my back deck looking over the canyon,
This time is certainly no waste.

Before the sun comes up, it's so quiet out there.
The sights and sounds are pure.
Always my thoughts turn to family.
My love for them will endure.

Now a nice summer breeze has come this way,
Seems God has touched my face.
Reminded once again these blessings are from Him,
I'm so thankful for my special place.

Ben Hagins

THE SOWER

This parable is found in the books of Matthew, Mark, and Luke and covers the four areas where any message, sermon, or story will affect you. It's one of my favorites, and I hope these words of wisdom will speak to you.

God's message is the seed,
and it's scattered everywhere.
Four places it usually goes.
One is the hard path. It doesn't stay very long.
Where it lands nobody knows.
The second is rocky soil. It's hard to grow here,
And the roots don't go very deep.
In these rocks with very little water,
These seeds won't grow and be reaped.
The third place that the Word might go
Is on the thorny ground.
The cares of the world and pleasures of life
Will keep the Word from being found.
Finally, the parable concludes with the fourth place,
Where good soil is available to all.
It's up to you how you receive this message
About the seed and where it falls.

SALT AND LIGHT

Do you have power and authority like Christ?
Probably you don't have quite this much might.

Then read and study Matthew 5:13-14,
And become the salt and the light.

Don't hide yourself under a basket.
Go to the mountain and shine.

Then your good deeds will be witnessed by others.
You'll become a mighty branch on His vine.

Just be a lighthouse. Let your walk be your talk.
Your influence will be seen by all.

Then you'll glorify your Lord
by serving your fellow man.
That's answering your Master's call!

Ben Hagins

SEVEN GIFTS

In the book of Romans, chapter twelve, the apostle Paul writes about seven gifts or traits given to Christ's followers. They are listed in verses six through eight, as follows:

1—Speaking

2—Serving

3—Teaching

4—Encouraging

5—Giving

6—Leading

7—Kindness

And while you're reading this chapter, please reflect on all twenty-one verses. I have underlined each of these and have even written this chapter out as a prayer.

See my thoughts on Romans 12—in my own words.

SEVEN GIFTS

What are the gifts that you've been given?
What example should you be?
Are you a **_speaker_** or do you **_serve_** others,
Maybe a **_teacher_** for all to see?

How about just being a very cheerful **_giver_**,
Encouraging others when seeing a need?
Don't squander your talents.
Be a **_leader_** and always **_kind_**.
Are these traits to which you agree?

Reflect on these seven gifts,
examining each as it fits your life
To see what you are to do.
And if you do these and follow Paul's words,
You'll discover the best gift for you.

Ben Hagins

SERMON ON THE MOUNT

Here are the twenty topics from chapters five through seven in Matthew:

1. Beatitudes

2. Salt and light

3. Fulfillment of the law

4. Murder

5. Adultery

6. Divorce

7. Oaths

8. Eye for an eye

9. Love your enemies

10. Giving to the needy

11. Prayer

12. Fasting

13. Treasures in Heaven

14. Do not worry

15. Judging others

16. Ask, seek, and knock

17. Narrow and wide gates

18. True and false prophets

19. True and false disciples

20. Wise and foolish builders

There you have it—twenty different topics from the Sermon on the Mount, sermonettes that Jesus taught from a mountainside overlooking the Sea of Galilee. The conclusion of these teachings states that Jesus taught as one who had authority, and the crowds were astonished.

These chapters are three of my favorites.

SERMON ON THE MOUNT

Made time this morning to read three chapters
About the Sermon on the Mount.

Chapters five through seven
from the book of Matthew
111 verses are the count.

It covers twenty topics about being blessed
And truths about what to do.

Wonder how many folks will take the time?
This choice is definitely up to you.

So glad I did—read and study these words.
We're taught that He is the way.

My challenge to you—be amazed by His teachings!
Now that's what happened today.

Ben Hagins

THE GOOD SAMARITAN

What a story we have
about a man with some problems—
Robbed, beaten, and left for dead.

Three came by, and two didn't help.
But the Good Samaritan responded,
and then Jesus said,

"Who was neighborly? Who loved God?
Who had mercy on him?"

Not the priest, or the Levite.
It wasn't either of them.

The bottom line is this: Love with your Heart,
Soul and Mind. Not much else is left.

Just follow this commandment.
There is nothing greater than this,
Love your neighbor as yourself!

T,U&V

Ben Hagins

THOUGHTS AND PRAYERS

What is your response
When a friend has a problem?
Usually, it is this that you say:

"I'm thinking of you
With my thoughts and prayers.
Is there anything I can do today?"

But let's be truthful,
We're not in their shoes.
It's just hard to know what to do.

Their adversity is real
and they need some support.
The answer—It just might be—YOU

To provide a listening ear,
And give the most precious thing there is.
It's called—TIME—and an understanding heart.

So next time you learn
About a friend in need—
Take action—and then do your part.

THE TWELVE

Before Jesus chose his twelve, He did it this way.
When He got by himself, He took the time to pray.

Now it was time to pick His men.
Two were named Simon and two were called Jim.

They were all tough, and always pretty handy
Another three were named—Phil, Tom, and Andy.

But always a requirement was to follow Jesus' heart.
The next three were called -- Matt, John, and Bart.

Now we're left with two. Can't put this off till later.
Both were named Jude, and one was a traitor.

I know this poem puts on a different spin.
These disciples became apostles, and all were in
God's plan.

NOTE: I'm sure you haven't thought of the twelve
disciples in this manner, and I wanted to add a
different spin to these remarkable followers of Jesus.

TIM PHILPOT

Over ten years ago, Tim Philpot and I met at a Links Players golf outing at the Prairie Club Golf Resort in remote Valentine, Nebraska.

I had recently helped to start our local chapter of Links Fellowship in Waco, Texas, because of the positive influence of David Cook and his book, <u>Seven Days of Utopia</u>. Accompanying me on this golf outing was my good friend and golfing "podnah," Rich Giles. Our hosts were Tim and the regional Links leader, Randy Wolff, who was most helpful in our making this trip work and our local fellowship get started.

Both Tim and Randy were true servants of the Lord and most influential in my development with Links Players. Tim's dad was an evangelist and camp meeting preacher in Kentucky where Tim later had an "Asbury Revival" experience.

Tim loves God and golf and was a golf letterman at the University of Kentucky about the same time I was at Baylor. Time wears Kentucky blue like I were Baylor green. Tim was also a family court lawyer and judge for fifteen years and was president of CBMC, Christian Business Men's Connection for seven years.

Last year, I had the privilege and opportunity to go with Tim to Ireland and Scotland to play the famous courses at Dornoch and Brora where Time does much of his book and devotional writings. His recent outstanding book, <u>Player's Progress</u>, is patterned after John Bunyan's, <u>Pilgrim's Progress.</u>

Tim was our keynote speaker at our local chapter's "end of the year" meeting in November of 2022. Thank you, Tim, for your words of wisdom for all of us at Waco Links Players Fellowship.

You're one of my favorites!

Ben Hagins

TRIBUTE TO TEACHERS

I'm reflecting this morning
On a springtime April day,
Watching buses drop off students
As our teachers make their way

To answer their call of duty
And educate young minds.
Their faithful and dedicated service
Are but two of the many signs

That describe to all that care,
The many things they do.
Following a regimented schedule,
Does that apply to you?

Probably not, unless your job
Is a calling, like many preachers.
If you can read and write,
Say a prayer for—and thank all your teachers!

TEACHERS—WHAT DO THEY MAKE?

All the schools in Texas
Will begin their classes soon!
Guess that's pretty smart,
So they'll finish before next June.

But, you ask, just what
Does a teacher make?
Well, not enough money—
A fact for heaven's sake.

But, here are the answers
To that question so real.
They make their students read,
Write, and think. Does that appeal

As a vocation to pursue
When discipline is an issue?
It is a worthy mission,
Just don't forget your tissue

'Cause this career is honorable,
And I'll tell you what it takes:
Many dedicated teachers
And the difference that they make!

Ben Hagins

TOMORROW'S WORLD

Is Social Security insecure?
Do we care about Medicare?
How high will the ceiling of debt be raised?
These government plans—we all share

In the form of taxes, about half of us pay,
Yet Congress spends more than they make.
Will our leaders truly be public servants, or just
feather their nests and take

Pay raises each year and trips to and fro?
Pretty soon we'll all be broke.
Now I'm telling the truth, better watch these trillions,
Or we're headed to becoming poor folk.

But let's get serious and use common sense.
We're a land of the free and the brave.
Better pay our troops that provide liberty,
and not forget the lives many gave

To give all opportunity to do as we wish.
Don't take for granted that this should be—
What we did yesterday, determines today, the world
tomorrow that we'll see!

VETERANS DAY

On the eleventh of November,
Veteran's Day we observe.
But recent events have made us cry.
In years long ago, our troops paid the price
For our freedoms, and now I ask why

Did so many before us go in harm's way
To serve the nation they love?
They did it for family, country, and freedom
And the right to worship the one above.

Now let me ask you what road you are on?
Just what destination is your quest?
Do you have a mission and purposeful goal
For life, liberty and happiness?

Now don't forget the privileges you have.
If you do, you'll have some regrets.
Just put your God first, then others second,
And, that date, remember our Vets!

Ben Hagins

VENUS

Up early today, enjoying my first cup of coffee on my back porch that faces south in Waco. The morning sky is especially tranquil during this time of worldwide crisis and pandemic virus.

The planet Venus, currently, is the "morning star." She rises in the southeast and is radiant at this moment. Equally stellar is the view from my Slice of Heaven retreat near Lake Whitney, as my back deck faces northwest and allows me to see this magnificent object as the "evening star." It is this month that Venus will be the brightest object in the night sky, second only to the moon.

Please enjoy my poetic version of Venus. It's one of my favorites.

VENUS

Venus and your beauty,
Oh, how bright you are today.

Mere words cannot tell
What the ancients tried to say.

Venus, in this early morning sky,
Heralding God's eternal story,

Proclaiming heaven's handiwork,
Displaying her power and glory.

Ben Hagins

VALLEY OF ELAH

I watched an interesting movie—The Valley of Elah, made in 2007, starring Tommy Lee Jones. Of course, I was familiar with the story of David and Goliath, but not familiar with where this battle took place.

Rereading the entire chapter 17 of 1 Samuel, I researched the background of the movie. I now know that this title can represent a place where conflict and resolution in one's life can be faced and found.

The principle was made clear at the movie's conclusion when an upside - down flag was symbolically shown to mean, "We're in distress. We don't know what we're doing. Please come help us."

Young David acted when he answered the call—in the Valley of Elah.

VALLEY OF ELAH

Only two times is this valley mentioned
in 1 Samuel, chapter 17.
Its name is Elah, where a battle took place
with a giant bigger than you have ever seen.

Of course, I'm talking about the story
that you've heard early in your years.
A young shepherd boy named David,
fought nine-foot Goliath, and did so with no fears.

For forty days, the Philistine army
challenged the Israelite men.
The enemy asked, "Who will represent you
to fight our giant, and just who will you send?"

When young David heard this, he said to Saul,
"With the Lord's help, I will go and fight.
I've been delivered from the lion and the bear,
and Goliath is the one I will smite."

The story ends in the Valley of Elah.
David accepted this challenge alone.
The head of Goliath was taken as predicted,
and the youth did it with a sword and one stone.

Ben Hagins

W

Ben Hagins

WHAT GOD WANTS YOU TO DO

Do you know God's will, right now for your life?
Just exactly what you are to do?
I know the answer is probably—no,
But the solutions rest entirely with you.

Reading a daily devotional, being faithful in the Word
Rising early is preferred by me.
For I find that such time, with coffee in hand,
Works best in my day to see

His wonders, His beauty, the majesty of it all.
It's too much to believe it just evolved.
For it took a Creator and faith on your part,
And your problems, yes, they can be solved

By the One who made it all.
Yet the skeptics still ask who?
Just be prepared to lead and help others
Know what God wants you to do.

WISE AND FOOLISH BUILDERS

If you read Jesus' words and put them into practice,
You will become a very wise man.

Your home will be built on the solid rock,
And not on the shifting sand.

For when the winds blow, and the rivers start to rise,
And the storms of life come your way,

You won't be foolish, but well prepared.
Your foundation will be firm that day.

After this sermon in only six verses,
Jesus had completed his speaking.

What a lesson to remember, this truth is so clear,
By the Master and His wise teaching.

Note: Matthew 7:24-29.

Ben Hagins

WHEN PLANS GO AWRY

A round of golf was planned by our group today. Guess what—it didn't happen. Seems that springtime will bring unexpected weather that takes control of everything. Like we were taught in the original Boy Scouts—

"Be Prepared."

Some favorite verses of mine are Proverbs 3:5-6. Your paths will be made straight when you acknowledge your Lord.

What happens when a rain washes away your day,
And the intentions that you've made? You really have
no say,

But a recipe for problems is to never plan ahead.
In Proverbs 3:5-6, that is what it said.

Just know there's no need to ask the question why.
You can count on this. Your plans can go awry!

WISDOM

If you want wisdom,
It's in the book of James,
Chapter one, verse five, to be exact.

Just ask your God in faith,
Without any doubt.
Then wisdom will be given, and that's a fact!

His practical advice
Is yours for asking.
Don't be like a wave in the sea,

But be stable in your ways.
Your Lord is a giver.
Isn't this true, and do you agree?

Ben Hagins

WICKER CHAIR

My mom, Lucie Hagins, died in my arms on Palm Sunday, 16 March, 2008, at the age of 89. We had received a call that she had fallen, not doing well, and was in the hospital in her hometown of Fordyce, Arkansas.

After settling her estate and going through her things, we decided that her old wicker chair, which was near and dear to her, would be a keepsake. Mom would love to sit on her front porch in that chair every morning before beginning her duties as church secretary.

My son Trey, at the time, had recently applied to Baylor and secured a position with University Development that required some travel. He asked Kathy and me to move to Waco and help with their young kiddos. We were so happy to do so, and got there within six months. Needless to say, Mom's wicker chair came with us.

Thank you, Sherri Cherry, for helping to get her old wicker chair repaired so we can enjoy it on our back deck.

WICKER CHAIR

I have an old wicker chair
That is very special to me.
Came from my Mom after she died.
Great memories I have are the key.

I so look forward
With my coffee in hand
As I sit in it and reflect.
Someday I will understand

The deep love she gave to me
And the way to treat people I meet;
It all helped me as I matured.
Everyone said Mom was mighty hard to beat.

So, I will end with this—
With Mom, there was none to compare.
And I think I'll appreciate this even more,
When I sit in her old wicker chair.

Ben Hagins

WHERE'S DAD?

Another special time we all enjoyed
During Thanksgiving season this year,
Food, football, and fellowship we had
Because the whole family was here.

But most unique was the little man, age seven,
My grandson—a challenge he can be!
Let's hike, start a fire, always wanting my time.
There's a lesson here, can't you see

That this ingredient is still the missing link
In half the families of this land?
Those absentee dads, what is their story,
Just why aren't they—the man

To lead their families and provide for them?
I'm not one to judge, but it's sad.
I just want them to know I'm so proud,
That my grandson has the best dad!

WHY DO I LOVE YOU?

Why do I love you?
I can mention several ways.
I've done so for over fifty years,
That's almost 20,000 days!

And when I slow down,
I think about you even more.
You are my gift from God,
And it's you who I adore.

I'm thankful you gave me our son,
And this time with both our grands.
You followed me to Texas,
And adopted my school in Waco land.

Now in this phase of life,
We can go to our lake retreat.
It's called our "Slice of Heaven,"
And together—worthy to repeat!

Ben Hagins

WONDERFUL LIFE

The movie, It's a Wonderful Life, is a 1946 Christmas supernatural drama film. It is based on a short story and booklet, The Greatest Gift.

The movie was unpopular in the beginning. When the copyright expired, the movie entered the public domain. It soon became the classic it is and starred Jimmy Stewart as George Bailey, under the direction of Frank Capra.

In the mid 1940's, George contemplates suicide, but his guardian angel saves George. When George says he wishes to have never been born, the story is replayed, showing what life was like without him.

Finally, George prays for his life back and says, "Please, God, let me live again." His wish is granted. George is then reunited with his family and townspeople, and the angel gives him a book with these words inscribed, "Remember, no man is a failure who has friends. Thanks for the wings."

What a tremendous movie and message, just like a life with Christ. Please enjoy my poem about a wonderful life. It's one of my favorites.

WONDERFUL LIFE

What a movie I look forward to
During every Christmas season!
Parallels of Jesus' life
Is the message and the reason

This film is so meaningful,
A classic for all to see.
Make it a family affair,
And I think you'll agree.

A fulfilled life you can have,
Just make a decision to give
Not for self, but for others to serve.
The abundant and wonderful life you'll live.

WHY NOT NOW?

Let's talk about procrastination. Well, maybe not. I can get to this later. Simply put, this habit of procrastination is defined as an act of delaying or putting off tasks until the last minute or even past a deadline.

Researchers say it's a failure in self-regulation leading to negative consequences. One study found that seventy-five percent of college students were habitual procrastinators.

I have personally found that using a daily "to-do" list helps me. I just put a box next to the item and look forward to putting a check mark in the box.

A close friend of mine reminded me of one of my favorite sayings, "Why not now?" He was helping me with some projects, and when I delayed, he stopped and said, "Why not now?" He waited for my reply. I looked at him and said, "You're absolutely right."

Shortly thereafter, the job was accomplished. I felt so good and wrote this poem as a reminder for me and others. It is one of my favorites.

WHY NOT NOW?

Have you ever heard a saying
That wouldn't leave your mind,
And it seemed to apply every day

To work or home chores
'Cause usually it's both?
Seems it's easier to look the other way

And put off till tomorrow
What you should do today.
You know what's the right thing to do.

For when you've accomplished
But the simplest of tasks,
It creates opportunities anew.

You just can't finish
The things you don't start.
I know you're wondering just how

Will I ever get things done
And reach my goals?
Just answer this question—WHY NOT NOW?

Ben Hagins

WHAT DID YOU LEARN TODAY?

I have always been learning and trying to teach my son and grandkids valuable lessons of life.

Since my college days, I developed the habit of note-taking and journaling. This led me to say this short question to my son and his friends, usually after a sermon, speech, or a class.

I would always get a wry look or comment, like—"Oh no, Mr. Hagins again!" But I had many good times and discussions with all his many friends throughout high school, college, and beyond.

Now, I'm doing just this with my grands, and now they are young adults, but it's me who now asks the questions, such as, "Why can't I get this computer to work?" Their usual response is, "What did you learn today? Look it up!"

I have a little question
And this is what I say—
As you travel along the road of life,
What did you learn today?

WHAT'S NEXT LORD?

Lord, help me know what's next for my life.
It's my prayer right now for me and my wife.

You've provided for us in each and every way.
I want to seek Your guidance
because You have the final say.

Not my will, but Thine. It's not always clear
Which path to take. Your presence will be near.

If I just listen to You and not rely on me,
The answer will be given, and I will then see

The direction I should go, the things I should do
As I plan for tomorrow by trusting in You!

X, Y & Z

Ben Hagins

YOU

At our Slice of Heaven place, close to Whitney Lake,
I've just built my day's first fire.
The morning is cold. The coffee is hot.
This scene I've just got to admire.

Blessed are my thoughts,
as I'm reflecting about friends.
But I'm also a little sad.
Some classmates I've lost, I've been told.
Now tell me something that will make me glad

To reminiscence about what it means to have a
common bond—
Be it church, sports, or something new.
When all is said and done,
just know this fact from me:
There's just something I like about you.

YES, HONEY

Learn from past mistakes and listen to this advice.
Be kind to your lady. It's pretty easy to be nice.

For it's very selfish to try and get your way.
But if trouble is what you want,
just ignore what I will say.

Here's that little tip, that will keep you "in the good."
And don't forget this lesson, not that you ever would.

Two words—say them often. I'm not being funny!
Do you want peace in your family?
Just say—Yes, honey!

Ben Hagins

ABOUT THE AUTHOR

 Ben Hagins grew up in the small town of Fordyce, Arkansas. He attended Baylor University and was Captain of his Golf Team. Ben graduated in 1970 with a major in Economics and was active in the Alpha Kappa Psi fraternity.

Ben then joined the U.S. Air Force, serving ten years, mostly in the B-52 program at Carswell Air Force Base in Fort Worth, Texas.

Upon his Air Force separation, due to the tragic death of his dad, Ben joined First Command Financial Planning and completed almost thirty years working with thousands of military families in the areas of savings, insurance, and investments.

Ben and his wife, Kathy, now spend their retirement years between Waco, Texas, and their "Slice of Heaven" home on Lake Whitney, Texas, near their son Trey, his wife Liz, and their children Robert and Kate.

Ben Hagins

ACKNOWLEDGMENTS

To my wife, Kathy, who reviewed the complete manuscript. She always gave me constructive critiques on grammar and content. I usually followed her recommendations, but she consented to certain areas for my various stories and poems. Kathy, my honey, "You're the best !"

I also must say thanks to my ten-year plus association with the Waco Christian Writers Workshop. This group was originally led by Reita Hawthorne and now led by Michelle Ruddell and Linda Hammond. Michelle tirelessly assisted me with computer issues and items that I just didn't understand.

Recently, a heartfelt thank you to Becky Armstrong, a retired English teacher, who in only two days read and critiqued my book with outstanding recommendations. And to Shantana Dodge for her help in overcoming my typing issues.

Additionally, I must say a big thank you to my publishing team at the Roaring Lambs organization. I distinctly remember attending a Saturday workshop years ago in Dallas with every intention of skipping the afternoon session and playing golf. I was so impressed with Donna Skell's leadership and the speakers' lineup that I canceled my recreation plans and "soaked it all in" at the workshop.

Then, because of the expertise of Roaring Lambs leaders like Frank Ball, Belinda McBride, Lisa Worley, and all workshop presenters, this book came to fruition.

Finally, a double-big thank you to my Director of Publishing, Marji Laine, who oversaw my work to completion. Her coaching, design, editing, formatting, and marketing tips made this book happen in a timely and financially doable manner. And Marji, when I said thank you, your response was never, "no problem, but always-no worries."

Marji, I'm also glad, you always found "a new favorite" when you reviewed and edited this book. Many thanks!

Ben Hagins

SPECIAL PEOPLE
WHO ARE MENTIONED IN THIS BOOK

Agatha Christie
Albert Schweitzer
Art Sticklin
Barbra Smith
Becky Armstrong
Belinda McBride
Benny Cherry
Candy Wagner
Charlie Hagins
Charlotte Heathcott
Cindy Potts
David Cook
Darryl Lehnus
Dick Couey
Don Anderson
Don Heathcott
Donna Skell
Edie Guffin
Ernest Hemingway
Francis Scott Key
Frank Capra
Franklin D. Roosevelt
Franklin Potts
Gil Strickland
Greg Laurie
James Dobson

Janet Dorrell
Jeff Price
Jeff Watters
Jerry Wagner
Jim Gates
Jim Huffhines
Jimmy Dorrell
Jimmy Stewart
John Grisham
Johnny Cash
Judy Huffhines
Joyce Kilmer
Kate Hagins
Kathy Hagins
Keith Mikeska
Linda Hammond
Linda Sands
Lisa Beamer
Lisa Worley
Liz Hagins
Lucie Hagins
Maddi Mosler
Marji Laine
Martin Luther
Michelle Ruddell
Mike McGraw

Mike Toby
Og Mandino
Paul Newman
Paul Sands
Pearl Anderson
Randy Marshall
Randy Wolff
Reita Hawthorne
René Maciel
Rich Giles
Robert Hagins
Robert Lewis
Rudyard Kipling
Sarah Price
Sherri Cherry
Stephen King
Terry Cosby
Tim Philpot
Todd Beamer
Tom Hagins
Tom Potts
Tommy Lee Jones
Trey Hagins
Vaughn Monroe
Vince Clark
Warren Guffin

228

I'm So Glad I Know!

I'm reflecting about my family from the back deck of my lake home. A cool rain has just come through the canyon and the sights and sounds of this setting are awesome. It's also tranquil, and my mind has turned to events of this last year and the past.

Mom died recently. My dad is gone also, having been killed in a tragic shooting accident thirty years ago. So why do I write this introductory narrative? To simply say,

I'M SO GLAD I KNOW ABOUT:

• THE FAMILY HISTORY:

Mom grew up on a plantation in the south. Those stories of her parents and siblings are near and dear to me. As is the story of when she came to the city and fell in love with the cute "soda jerk" behind the drugstore counter. The many pictures of them, and the war years resulted in stories that are so meaningful to me.

I'M SO GLAD I KNOW ABOUT MY FAMILY'S HISTORY!

• THE ACCOMPLISHMENTS:

I wrote my Mom's obituary. I'm so glad I knew of her many accomplishments for her church and community. She was somewhat a packrat, having saved numerous articles about church and civic activities. She was a doer, and so was my Dad, a pillar in his city, a honest and disciplined businessman and an example to many.

I'M SO GLAD I KNOW ABOUT MY PARENTS' ACCOMPLISHMENTS!

• THE FINANCIAL AFFAIRS:

Dad didn't make that much money but we never did without. He provided for us and my college years in ways I later learned about. He meticulously wrote down where the money was and would come from should anything happen. He even outlined the maintenance schedule for the car and home items. This left Mom and I very comfortable.

I'M SO GLAD I KNOW ABOUT THEIR FINANCIAL AFFAIRS!

My point to this article is:
If you don't know certain things about your family history, your parents' achievements, and their financial affairs, then make the time to do so.

You'll be glad you did, and so will your children and grandchildren.

I'M SO GLAD I KNOW!

Ben Hagins

Ben Hagins

Made in the USA
Columbia, SC
15 September 2024

41781386R00126